CAN'T LET NOBODY
RIDE MY BIKE

Robert Mossi Alexander

Can't Let Nobody Ride My Bike

Cover image: © Sam Smith

Published by Chocolate Readings via KDP Publishing

www.chocolatereadings.com

ISBN-13: 9781795163927

Publisher's Note

The advice and strategies contained herein may not be suitable for your situation. You should consult a professional where appropriate. Neither the publisher nor the author shall be liable for any damages arising here from.

Dedication

I would like to dedicate this book to my children, whom I call the elements: **Earth, Air, Fire, and Water.**

Lauryn, I named you **Earth,** because when you were born, I was determined to protect you. The human race has not done a good job of protecting and taking care of Mother Earth, but as your father, I will ensure your safeguarding and preservation.

To my oldest son, Robbie, you are the **Air** that I breathe. You gave my life purpose and direction. You being born was like a breath of fresh air to the lungs of an asthma sufferer.

Jaylen, you are the **Fire** that keeps our family going. Fire brings warmth and that is what you do for the Alexander clan. When you were born premature, the fire inside of you would not die and allow you to leave this world.

Isaiah, you are **Water** in the purest form. You mean so much to me. Just like human beings need water to survive, I need you in my life to survive in this crazy world.

Lauryn, Robbie, Jaylen, and Isaiah, I love you and dedicate this to you.

Preface

I want to thank everyone who purchased this book or borrowed it from someone to read. Who says black folks from the hood don't read? As an avid reader and writer, I felt it was imperative for me to get my story out.

This is a memoir based on me growing up in Oakland, California. As an Oakland native, and son of a writer and librarian, I felt the need to express how growing up in East Oakland after the heroin epidemic and during the crack era shaped my life for the better, in spite of the environment.

This book represents the lives of many black boys living in ghettos throughout the United States. I want to inspire young black boys to be creative with their writing and let them know they are not alone. I want them to know it's okay to be intelligent and go after your dreams.

My childhood experiences taught me that if you are a good person, no matter the environment, that goodness will shine through. They say cream rises to the top, and that's what growing up in Oakland showed me.

There are several chapters throughout the book that should resonate with you no matter what hood or city you grew up in. When faced with decisions in life, it is crucial to understand how these decisions may impact you short-term and long-term, positively and negatively, or morally and immorally. Specifically, as a young African American male, you will be faced with many challenges or decisions that will shape you, guide you, and potentially change you. There is no prescription to becoming a man. You keep being tested, and God willing, you make it to adulthood. Overcoming obstacles is an easy way to say it, but some would say, survival of the fittest.

If we look at a young male's development from a biological standpoint, scientists and brain researchers have figured out that the area of the brain responsible for how decisions are made is the prefrontal cortex (PFC). The prefrontal cortex is located at the front of the frontal lobe. Women can experience a fully developed prefrontal cortex by the age of twenty-one, while men don't experience a fully developed prefrontal cortex until the age of twenty-five. Not only is the prefrontal cortex responsible for how we make decisions, but it also affects our personality development, planning, and how we navigate our social expression.

While writing this book, I wanted to be as honest as possible in terms of how my early decisions were made without a fully developed PFC. With this new knowledge of the PFC or information that has been reiterated about your own underdeveloped PFC, look back at your life. Most folks can clearly think of instances when they should have never dated him or her, or should have never gotten in that car, or should have gone right instead of left.

Everything is clear when you are looking through the rear-view mirror, but when you experience these decision-making moments in real time, your vision is hazy. This is an explanation as to why:

People have asked me, "Why did you choose Oakland as the setting for your memoir?" I love Oakland and what

Oakland represents, from *The Mack* being filmed in West Oakland to the revolutionary Black Panthers.

I bought my home in Oakland because every single time I drive, bike, or walk through "The Town," I am reminded of my amazing childhood.

I imagine the similarities between Oakland and other urban cities around the country, like Detroit, Chicago, New York, Compton, and Los Angeles. Apparently, I am not the only one in love with Oakland, because if that was the case, gentrification would not be as big of an issue as it is today. But I'm in love with old Oakland.

As I go through life as an educator who has worked most of my life in Silicon Valley, I meet people from all walks of life. I have met people who have visited Oakland and love it. On the flip side, I have met people who have come to Oakland on the weekend and had a horrible experience.

The people I am most intrigued by are the folks who have never been to Oakland but judge The Town based on what they see in the news or horror stories they've heard from other people. Like my father would say, "If you go out looking for trouble, trouble will find you."

Some of my childhood friends who are no longer here were out looking for trouble. It was a self-fulfilling prophecy. You will get what you put into the universe. If you are constantly trying to better yourself and you are on a mission to be a successful contributing member to society, then that will happen. You put those good thoughts into the atmosphere and watch your positive ideas emerge. But if you are constantly playing "the world is against me" card, then negative things will manifest. It will seem like the world is always against you because this is what you put out into the universe and what you expect.

My book addresses issues that revolve around violence, drugs, and teen sex. Since these things were prevalent all throughout my childhood and teenage years, it was essential for me to address these experiences. I didn't want to be like the people who preach abstinence, knowing full well that teenagers can and will have sex. My goal is to highlight how unprepared and uninformed many youth are when it comes to sex and address how we can prepare our youth in the future to be better informed and make better choices in particular circumstances.

I also address gang culture and turf wars, since they were things that I survived and were unavoidable. It is hard to tell someone who never experienced the urban city what brotherhood is like when it comes to survival and what to do. How can you explain to someone that being in a gang might kill you, but it can also save your life? The Yin and the Yang is in almost every aspect of life. The interconnectedness and the contrast have always been important, and I have tried to convey that in this book.

This is what rapper MC Eiht wrote:

I gotta another gang story to tell

Peep, about how a black brotha was born in hell

And right then and there it's no hope

Cause a brotha can't escape the gangs and dope, Damn!

And when it's black on black that's a pity

Can't survive in the Compton City

And fool that's a bet

Cause when you grow up in the hood, you gots to claim a set

Yeah, it's not that you want to but you have to

Don't be a mark cause brothas might blast you!

—"Hood Took Me Under," **MC Eiht**

MC Eiht not only describes the gang culture, but also how it was almost mandatory for his survival. His version is extreme, and just like anything else, you have to form your own opinion.

This verse is another way of using music to make a connection or drive home a point. I use music all the time when I'm teaching and however the connection is made through examples, scenarios, short stories, and music, then so be it.

The soundtrack to an East Oakland Childhood was important for me to include because I believe music puts you in a particular state of mind. I can remember where I was the first time I heard Run DMC, The Fat Boys, Slick Rick, Doug E Fresh, Big Daddy Kane, and Rakim and Heavy D.

I remember dancing hard to MC Hammer and Kid 'n Play or doing the Humpty Dance at house parties just like Digital Underground. For instance, certain songs make me think of the spring season leading into the summer, and certain other songs made me appreciate hard times or burying a loved one. Groups like Public Enemy, Poor Righteous Teachers,

KRS-One, and X Clan taught me to be righteous and pro-black and still kick fresh rhymes.

Moreover, I added Bay Area rap verses to my story because they represent my hometown and things I experienced growing up. Bay Area rappers don't get enough credit as slang originators. Some of the most gifted MCs came from my soil, the Bay Area, including The Delinquents, Bad N-Fluenz, 3 X Krazy, Souls of Mischief, San Quinn, RBL Posse, The Luniz, Dru Down, C–BO, JT the Bigga Figga, Rappin' 4Tay, Andre Nickatina, the Mob Figaz. Pioneers like Digital Underground, The Coup, Conscious Daughters, MC Hammer, Too Short, E-40, and Rest in Power to Seagram Miller, Rappin' Ron, Mr. Cee, Mac Dre, Plan Bee, and the Jacka.

As founder and CEO of Hood to Higher Education, I want young boys and girls of color to know that there is no glass ceiling on what you can accomplish. You should not be afraid to be intelligent. You should not have to hide who you are. Be authentic, and most importantly, be yourself. I am working with the Bay Area Writers Project to help young aspiring writers create projects and find their voice.

There is much more to come. To be continued…

Chapter 1

The Sideshow

Straight lace Zeniths and vogues on a point
On my way to the Town to get a doja joint
Pushed it to the 7 to get some dank
Hit the liquor store to cold get drank
Now I got my doja, my drink is like Nitro
Peace, playboy, I'm on my way to the side show
Down Bancroft, to the light
Let me warm it up, I hit a donut tight
There's a Chevy on my side, windows straight tinted
I think he got hype when he saw me spin it
I'm up outta there, sideways to the next light
Vogues kinda smokin but Zeniths still tight

—"The Sideshow," **Richie Rich**

The sideshow: That was going to be ME at the intersection. Yeah, right there on the corner of 73rd and MacArthur. Everybody would be watching me in my dope ride and how I handle my vehicle with ease—with the greatest of ease, burning rubber, spinning doughnuts, throwing up my hood. The crowd was going crazy because they never saw a car with perfect candy paint, flawless leather interior, and the rims—oh the rims! Look how the gold-plated rims reflect off the sun.

Yeah, I thought, that's going to be me in three years. As soon as I get old enough to get my license, I'm going to save and get me a '68 Chevelle. No wait, a Cutlass Oldsmobile would make their mouths drop. Everybody knows a Mustang 5.0 is best for swinging doughnuts. But I saw this one dude in his fly Pontiac Lemans on rims. I could picture myself in a Cougar on Rally tires.

I was trying to calculate how much time I would have before the streetlight came on. On my block, if you were under sixteen, your parents would whip your tail if you were not in the house by the time the streetlights came on. I had roughly an hour judging where the sun was.

Falling deeper into my daydream, I heard Scooter trying to get my attention. "Hey Ron, that boy got handles, huh?"

Handles mean that the person driving has full control of the vehicle, the ability to drive the vehicle effortlessly. Being able to do doughnuts in a tight intersection is a skill. It is a skill I wanted to possess.

I yelled over the screeching tires, "Yeah he's dope, but almost lost control!"

See, you never want to stand too close to the corner because last year I heard a crowd was standing on 66th and Foothill (by the McDonald's) and dude did not have any handles, lost control of his ride, and smacked into a young lady, leaving her flat as a pancake.

Scooter and I watched from a distance. If we leaned against the wall and stood on the back of our bike pegs, we could see over the crowd.

It was Friday night and everybody and their mama was there. Well, everybody from our neighborhood, at least. There was Manny, James, Earl, Scooter, Tyrell, Tyreik (Tyrell's little brother), Victor, Michelle, Dee Dee, Porche, and of course Evelyn.

Evelyn was a work of art, the first black girl I ever seen with green eyes, smooth milk-chocolate skin with no flaws or blemishes. I mean Evelyn was *fine*, so fine she had brothas looking for her in the daytime with a flashlight.

Most of the kids my age rode their bikes everywhere, and if they didn't, they rode on the handlebars of their friends. I wondered if I was the only one thinking about the car I would one day be ripping the streets of Oakland up in.

I'm thirteen now, and if I start saving now, I could get my ride. I will get a work permit next year, so I can start working early. I'll show them. I already knew I got handles because I have practiced my skills on my go kart and at Malibu.

Not Malibu, California, with all the rich white people who have mansions right there on the beach, but Malibu Grand Prix on Hegenberger Road. Malibu Grand Prix has a baseball batting cage, video arcade, and go karts. The crew and

I went for the go karts. That's how I knew I could drive and was going to be a sideshow superstar. None of my friends could beat me racing go karts. Big cars couldn't be much different.

See, sideshows in East Oakland were a way of life; they were a place to showcase The Town's hottest rides. Oaktown has always been about high-performance cars. Forget that low-riding crap in Los Angeles. What can your vehicle do in an open space? I'm talking speed. Doughnuts! Figure-eights! You feel me!

Sideshows are spontaneous, too. They can start up right after the club lets out, or could just be some random dudes on the corner, yelling out, "Swing your shit!" or "What it do?" when they see you cruising the strip in your juiced-up whip.

"What it do?" was a challenge. It would be time to show The Town your ride and your skills. Never back down unless you want to be considered a scrub.

All of this swirling in my mind, and I'm taking in the whole scene, when I heard Victor tease Scooter, yelling out, "Hey Hook Head, don't you want to give me a ride home?"

The sideshow was on 73rd but we all lived on 78th. I could walk home in about 20 minutes, but a ride on the handlebars was 2 minutes. We often called Scooter "Hook Head" because the back of his head was shaped like Captain Hook's metal hook hand. Question Mark head was too long to say, but that's how it looked.

Scooter replied, "Shut up fool, and go get me a bean burrito, and hold the guac."

I heard a few girls giggle. Scooter was witty and a quick thinker. That is why I liked him and he was my best friend. Scooter had moved to 78th from 71st when he was eight years old. I was one year older. We got into a fight within two weeks of him living there. He was picking on my friend, Brandon, for no reason, and since I knew Brandon longer, I took his side. Scooter did not back down during the fight and made me instantly like and respect him.

In my neighborhood, fighting does not always solve problems, though. If you whip somebody, you have to worry about them coming back with a big brother or cousin to whip your butt. Or even worse, if they can't stomach the embarrassment of losing a fight and they go get a gun.

Victor was a good friend, too. He was a Mexican boy growing up in a mostly black neighborhood, so he had to be tough because he was different. He got picked on because he was different. He learned how to box because he was different. Victor was first-generation Mexican American. His parents did not speak any English. All they spoke was Spanish in the house. He got his street slang from the block. He had the best of both worlds.

"Which car was the tightest?" I asked. Scooter and Victor both looked to the clouds as if they were looking to the Lord up above for answers.

Scooter finally said, "That all-black Buick Grand National was ripping it up, blood! Did you see all that smoke? Looked like a freaking magic show!" I and Victor laughed at his metaphor.

"That baby-blue Camaro was too clean! I would love to have that!" Victor said with envy.

"Hell yeah!" Scooter and I said almost at the same time.

Scooter began grinning and said, "If ya'll lucky, I might let ya'll ride shotgun when my girl ain't with me. People often mistake her for Halle Berry, feel me?" Scooter was always taking a fantasy to the next level. He was the best when we played "What if." I was still scared of girls, so they were not on my radar.

All of a sudden, we saw three police cars driving fast down MacArthur with their sirens blasting. The gray Z28 IROC did a half doughnut and peeled off into the night, with two of the cop cars trailing from a distance.

The crowd was in a frenzy. Everybody started running and in no particular direction. It looked like more than three hundred people scrambling like roaches when the light came on. I heard that the cops could arrest you for being a bystander since sideshows are illegal.

One dude fell down during the chaos and you could hear people laughing as he picked himself up off the ground. Victor quickly jumped on Scooter's handlebars, and we sped down Hillside Street on our way home.

We thought we were professional bike riders. Our bikes were our cars. You wanted a bike that looked cool, but you also wanted that bike to be lightweight and built to last. The top bikes were BMX, Mongoose, or Redline. The last bike you would want to be seen on was a Huffy. The Huffy is notorious for falling apart. It was like having a Pinto as your car. It is not a matter of if but when you will have bike problems if your parents got you a Huffy.

I had a gray and black BMX and I kept it clean. Just like my future car, I had nice rims. They were called mags, and I would tell people if Batman had a bike, it would look just like this. I loved my bike and would put nothing before it.

I sped up as I heard the sirens get closer. I weaved in and out of the lanes and around people running. I swerved around parked cars, sometimes using the sidewalk when it was free and other times on the street. It was a sport to me and I was speed racer number one.

Tyrell was fifteen years old, but we were both in the eighth grade. Tyreik was Tyrell's little brother and a mini version. They both had no respect for authority. Tyrell had been held back a grade. He was the only one in junior high school who could grow a full beard. He loved giving younger kids hell and he was older and bigger than everyone in our grade. I saw him fumbling for his bicycle that was starting to be too small for him.

Tyrell and Tyreik lived on 77th in the Greenside Projects and would soon be heading the same direction I was. I did not want him to see me because I knew he would have something mean to say and I was too scared to say anything back, so I weaved around him while he was facing the other direction—close call.

Not too far from him, I saw Evelyn walking fast, trying to keep up with her best friend, Dee Dee. Dee Dee was short for Deidra. I had a set of pegs on my back wheel if she needed a ride. My handlebars were free, too. I should ask her if she needs a ride. Nobody would care because I was just being nice.

As I approached her, my little heart began to freeze up, and at the last minute, I yelled to Evelyn, "BE SAFE!" I always heard my Aunt Adrienne telling somebody that.

Dee Dee snarled back, "What are you, our grandma or something?!" I shook my head in embarrassment and kept going.

In my neighborhood, anybody could roast you and have you feeling like you were less than nothing. You couldn't show any pain or emotion. I learned that the hard way already.

Evelyn did not laugh or comment. She kept looking at me as she hopped on Dee Dee's handlebars. Maybe she thought that was nice of me and we could go to an eighth-grade dinner dance together.

As Evelyn and I were slow dancing in my fantasy, Scooter yelled, "Preacher Ron, come by my house in a couple of minutes and BE SAFE!" with a smirk on his face. I paid him no attention and proceeded to go to the liquor store for some Now & Laters candy.

Scooter and Victor kept going to their house. The liquor store closest to our house did not let you bring your bike in the store. I was always in and out because I didn't want my bike stolen and there was no place to lock up your bike in front of the store.

Behind the counter at the liquor store is the son of the owner that everybody in the neighborhood called Arab Arash. Now what is important to note is that in order for you to be an Arab you have to be from one of the Arabian countries. Arash and his family are from Pakistan, which made little difference to my hood.

"Can I get one pack of Watermelon and one pack of Apple?" I asked. He handed me the packs and gave me change without even looking in my direction.

"What are those cops doing heading that way? You and your boys broke into a car?" he asked.

"Nah man, just riding through, and folks started acting crazy in their cars," I replied, knowing deep down in my heart that I *loved* every minute of that craziness. I wanted to be in that craziness. Forget being in it, I wanted to be front and center of that craziness!

Something told me Arab Arash did not think highly of me and my friends, so I was outta there in 2 minutes or less and didn't even spend my whole dollar.

Scooter lived across the street and up the block. He was on the porch when I got to his place. "Wait here," he told me. He went into the house and returned with my Nintendo controller. I let him borrow it because I only needed one. My little sister Leah was five years old and too young to play. Scooter had three siblings and they were always competing with one another.

Scooter said, "My dad wanted me to give you your controller back before we broke it." Scooter's dad, Tony, was no joke. He was strict with Scooter and his brother and sisters because he wanted them to stay alive and not make mistakes that would ruin their lives. I have seen Tony give Scooter whippings in front of the whole neighborhood. It was a sport to him, and I thought it was competition between my dad and his dad on who gave the best butt whippings. They were gold medalists in butt whippings!

"Thanks man. That sideshow was sick! I thought somebody was going to get killed by the cars or the stampede at the end," I said, still full of excitement.

Scooter's face lit up as if he was replaying the swinging cars in his head.

"The weekend was over, and summer was just three weeks away. I kept reminding myself don't trip. I was trying to see a sideshow every day this summer," Scooter said in a wishful voice.

Just then, as I was getting ready to ask Scooter about the eighth-grade dinner dance, I noticed the street lamp beginning to flicker, and I panicked.

I told Scooter I will chop it up with him tomorrow and made a mad dash to the house. Even though I knew I am supposed to put my bike in the shed in my backyard, I didn't. I busted through the front door to show Moms and Pops I made a real effort to respect their wishes.

My dad was in the living room as soon as I walked in. "Boy, you playing with fire. You know that?" He said it more like a statement than a question.

"Sorry Dad—just got caught up talking to Scooter. That's all. I beat the streetlights though," I said triumphantly.

My father had a smirk on his face, so I knew he wasn't in a bad mood. He really was a good man, but the stress of his job sometimes made him take that stuff out on me. He would whip me for the smallest things. If he wasn't whipping me for something insignificant, he would be yelling at my mom, and she would take it...mostly.

"I know you and your knuckle-head friends were down there watching that damn sideshow. People get killed at those every weekend, but that don't stop you... No, you want to be like everybody else. Always want to be in the mix. You gonna find out the hard way, huh?"

"Dad, we just be hanging. Besides, all the neighborhood be down there. I'm being safe," I proclaimed, sounding cocky.

"Being safe? You ain't gonna say nothing when a Chevy Nova hops the curb and runs your narrow behind over, now will you? But you know everything, right?"

I watched as his mood and demeanor shifted. Leah peeked around the corner. She already had her pajamas on.

"Go to bed, princess. I'm talking to your brother right now."

My dad could go from zero to sixty miles an hour in a heartbeat. I knew not to test him or play with his intelligence. I knew when to agree with him to get out of trouble and when I had room to test boundaries. And this wasn't one of those times. I wasn't going to give him a reason to get his favorite leather belt. One time he said, "You know I whip you because I love you." I was thinking then you must love me to death.

"You are right, Dad. I have no reason being there," I said in agreement.

"You damn right I'm right. Now take out the trash and get ready for school tomorrow," he said, patting me on the head like I was a German shepherd. I headed straight to the kitchen to take out the trash and put my bike in the shed.

I laid out my clothes for tomorrow, took a quick shower, and brushed my teeth. My dad's words were still swimming in my head. He just wanted me to make sound decisions. Pops cared about me and that's why he was so hard on me. He saw too many teenagers die young and he didn't want that to happen to me. I wanted to make him proud, but I loved my friends and the streets, too.

I loved the time right before bedtime and right after I woke up in the morning, because it was just me and my thoughts: The sideshow was popping! Evelyn wanted me! My Cougar sitting on rims! What a day in East Oakland!

Just then, before I passed out, my mother peeked in the bedroom. "Good night, son," she said in her sing-songy voice.

She knew my dad already gave me an earful. "Good night, Ma," I said. She leaned forward and kissed me on the forehead. I wondered what my dreams had in store for me that night.

But I also couldn't stop thinking about the lyrics to Richie Rich's "Sideshow":

To stop the sideshow, officer, just think
Maybe you should come and hit the spot with a tank
Cause the brothers from the O are gonna keep on ridin'
Yolkin', hittin' tight ones, straight sidin'
See, we ain't really trippin' off jail or the tickets
A brother wants to post, make mail and kick it
Now listen, this is the code to the show
For the people out there who just don't know
If your car is real clean, then bring it

If it's high-performance, then swing it
If it's a motorcycle, you better serve it
And if you get a ticket, you better deserve it
As long as you can say, "Man, I let 'em know"
Then peace, you did it at the side show

—"Sideshow," **Richie Rich**

Chapter 2

The Eastmont Mall

So what happens when a people do not get they dues
Well, let' try it, there's a riot so flip on the news
And let's go reach the 98th here in Oaktown
But let's just say for story's sake that it's in your town
A hundred brothers takin' factories, Warren's law is gutters
And now they handin' out free chicken and free peanut
butter
Free food to the people, how it should be
But now let's go a few blocks over to seventy-three
Channel two says at the mall twelve cops got shot
'Cause there's eight hundred sistas takin' over Eastmont

—"Dig It," **Boots Riley (The Coop)**

The Eastmont Mall was located right in the heart of East Oakland. That is probably where the name originated. It ran between 66th and 73rd and it was the place to be! When I was a baby, my mom would walk me in my stroller from our house on 78th Ave. to Eastmont Mall and that did not change when I became a kid.

I remember when Mark Curry used to work at Thrifty's when I was five years old. Mark Curry was the man! He was an Oakland legend. He was a comedian who had his own TV show called *Hanging with Mr. Cooper.*

You could always see Bay Area rappers at Eastmont Mall too, like Too Short, The Delinquents, Dangerous Dame, Father Dom, and MC Pooh, to name a few.

It was Saturday morning. I heard a knock at the door, followed by the doorbell. "Who the hell is that this early in the morning?!" my dad howled out. It was probably Scooter, Manny, or Victor. "Go get the door!" my father beckoned to me.

I answered the door with sleep still in my eyes. "Hey, what's up?" I said. It was Scooter and Manny.

"Nothing man. You still in bed. We were going to ride our bikes to the mall when it opened. Wanna go?" Scooter asked.

"Yeah, maybe later. I have to do some chores and stuff." I could see the disappointment on their faces, but it was early and I had stuff to take care of around the house. "But maybe we could hit *The Gong Show!*" I knew this would get them excited.

The Gong Show was a big talent search competition. It was like a talent show, but they often had radio personalities, DJs, music producers, and big-time executives there. So folks were bringing their best skills to the stage or run the risk of being booed and a funny dude dressed like a clown would hit the Gong on you. It was embarrassing to the contestant, but hilarious to the onlookers.

Just then my dad came to the door and peered over my shoulders, "Who's there?" he said.

"Hi Mr. Anderson," my friends said reluctantly.

"Why do ya'll have to knock and ring the doorbell? One or the other is just fine. We *can* hear you, you know," he said.

It was early for a Saturday and my dad hated being woken up. I just hoped he didn't take it out on me.

"Sorry about that, Mr. Anderson. See you later, Ronald," Scooter said, putting on his speaking-to-adults voice.

We all had a different voice, tone, and demeanor when talking to parents. We didn't feel like it was phony, but it was something we would do out of respect for our elders. We ALL did it. My father rolled his eyes and walked away.

"Man, your dad be tripping! He be on your head like cheese on pizza," Manny said.

Manny only had his mom in the house and never met his dad. Manny could get away with more stuff than me because of it. I was jealous of the fact that Manny never had to answer to anybody but his mom, and his mom was rarely home.

"He be sweating me over the smallest things. I think he be stressed out over not getting a lot of hours for his job. Anyway, I should be out after breakfast. Don't go to Eastmont without me, bruh. Peace." I turned and went back in the house.

I poured a big bowl of Captain Crunch. Captain Crunch was my favorite cereal. If you did not eat it right after you poured the milk in, it would be Captain Soggy.

Most Saturdays my mom would cook eggs, bacon, and grits because we did not have enough time in the morning right before school. My mother and dad must have had an argument because my mom was not her normal cheerful self.

I got my bowl of cereal and parked myself right in front of the TV. One of my favorite cartoons, *Ducktales*, was just going off, but I could still watch *Thundercats*. Watching cartoons was fun because it allowed me to escape my little kid problems for a short moment.

After I ate and watched cartoons for a bit, it was time to knock out these chores. I had to sweep the kitchen and bathroom floors, wipe down the countertops, and mop. I liked to whistle while I worked. Shout out to Snow White and the Seven Dwarfs.

My mother showed me how to sweep and mop. My mom and dad both felt that this taught a kid responsibility. Sometimes I wondered if my mom and dad had me just so I could do chores. I was good at it, too. I only had to wash dishes once a week and that was usually on Sundays.

My sister Leah came into the kitchen because she heard me whistling. I could tell she wanted to help, so I showed her how to wipe the counter. She was happy to be helping her big brother.

I would imagine what it would be like to be a slave doing these chores for the white man. If you didn't do these chores well enough or fast enough, the slave master would whip your butt. I know I could not have lived back then because I wasn't tough enough. I was sensitive, and if I didn't like getting a whipping from my parents, just imagine how I would react to a leather whip ripping my skin open.

This is something that black people often thought about. I wondered if white kids ever had these thoughts—probably not.

My parents wanted me to focus on my schoolwork. They were always preaching the importance of college. I kind of liked school, but most of my friends hated it.

"Hey Mom, can you look at the floors? I did a good job, huh?" I said rather cockily, trying to get her to lighten up. As she looked around at the kitchen floor, her face began to form a half smile.

"Yes, baby. You did a great job. Are you going outside with your friends? It looks like the weather is going to be gorgeous."

The weather was always nice in Oakland. Never much cooler than 70 degrees and the only thing we had to worry about during the winter was rain. I often wondered what it would be like to have a "snow day" like on the East Coast. I would never complain about missing school.

"Yeah Mom, we're gonna ride our bikes to Eastmont. Maybe hang out till *The Gong Show* comes on," I said.

"Have fun, don't get into any trouble, and don't let NOBODY ride your bike."

"I won't, Mom. Thanks."

Letting someone ride your bike in the hood was a big risk. It was a risk because someone could break it, or even worse, steal it, and never bring it back. Your bike was your car in the hood. Whoever got you that bike intended on *you* riding it, and *not* the whole neighborhood.

I got dressed and grabbed my bike from the back. I rode down 78th Ave. to where the crew was. They were hanging out, sitting on the back of Mr. Black's camper. That was our chill spot.

"Thought you would never finish," Scooter said.

"I know, bruh. I thought the weekends are supposed to be your days off?" I said, with a confused look on my face.

"Did you hear all that shooting last night? I heard some dude got popped on Greenside," Manny said. Manny always seemed to have the 411 on what was going on in the hood.

You had to worry about getting your butt whipped by other kids or your parents. You also had to worry about being in the wrong place at the wrong time and getting shot. My father used to say, "Son, a bullet ain't got no name." And that meant anybody could be shot and killed by a stray bullet.

"Nah, I didn't hear anything. I was sleep by 10:30 p.m.," I said, disappointed.

"By 10:30 p.m.!" Manny said teasingly. "Did your mommy tuck you in too?!"

"Maybe yours would too if yo' mama was ever home. Don't be mad because your mama don't love you, scrub," I fired back.

The crew all said, "Aw, that was cold-blooded."

We called this "capping," or "dissing." Back in the day, it was called "playing the dozens." It was putting down someone based on information you knew about them. You had to be funny and you had to be quick-witted. The point was to get under someone's skin without being too personal. Oftentimes, going deep was the only way to get someone back. If somebody went on a personal attack, then you had permission to say whatever.

Victor grabbed his bike and the look on his face was that of someone in deep concentration. "Watch this!" he yelled at us. As he was riding, he leaned back and put one wheel in the air, balancing himself on the back tire. He popped a wheelie and kept it going all the way to the top of the block.

"That was fresh!" I said and attempted one myself.

I was fast on my bike, but was not great at popping a wheelie. We all took turns. We looked like a bunch of BMX tricksters and this was our show.

Victor was probably the best at it. Scooter and Manny were good, too. I was just okay at it. I thought since my bike was light that I could master this. We practiced for a couple hours and toward the end I was able to wheelie halfway up our block. I was getting better. Whenever a car came, we had to swerve out of the street or we'd get hit.

In front of Scooter's house was a faucet. The faucet was supposed to be hooked up to the hose, for watering the grass, but you couldn't tell five thirsty teenagers that. We all took turns sticking our head under the faucet, turning the lever and letting the cold water pour into our mouths. It was so cold and so refreshing.

After getting a drink, I yelled out, "Race you to the mall!"

Everyone made a mad dash for their bikes and raced toward Hillside Avenue. Hillside connected to the Eastmont Mall. It was a long stretch with no speed bumps and was perfect for racing.

I had the lead for most of the race, but just as we were about to pull into the parking lot, Scooter passed me. He had won. We didn't call him Scooter for nothing. He was hella fast. We always went into the entrance located by Mervyn's on the second floor.

We used two long locks to lock up all five of our bikes. We locked them to a pole right outside of Mervyn's. Eastmont was popping with people—some people shopping and some people getting some food from H Salt Fish and Chips or Las Palmas. The older fellas were hanging out trying to get a girl to talk with them.

The mall was a fun place because you could people-watch and see all walks of life. The young teenagers my age just wanted to be in the mix, the older teenagers were looking to find a date, the D Boys, or Dope Boys, were shopping for new clothes and kicks, and the older folks were shopping for household items.

Most people came to Eastmont to go shopping at JC Penny's, Mervyns, or Footlocker. T's Wauzi is where you went to get the fresh music. My dad took me to buy my first rap album there, *The Great Adventures of Slick Rick*. At T's Wauzi, Bay Area rappers would promote their albums, too.

Mr. Z's was the spot to get all your fresh gear. My crew and I could only afford what our parents bought us. My mother was always in Mervyn's or JC Penney's getting me some Wranglers or Toughskin jeans. On our feet, we wore Payless Shoes or Coaster Slip-Ons. We would even rock flip flops or Karate shoes from the flea market.

I would always see the D Boys in Mr. Z's. You could tell they were D Boys because of the shiny gold rope chain and the brick cellular phone that they were struggling to hold.

The D Boys around my way had matching Adidas tracksuits. They might be rocking some Troop, or polka-dot Blackmail, shirts. Depending on the flavor of the month, shoes like Diadoras, Pumas, Adidas, and Nike Air Jordan's were in demand. My crew could do nothing but dream about having these fly shoes. Our folks did not buy us any of that stuff.

We were not there to shop, or eat, or talk to girls. We just wanted to see some people get booed at *The Gong Show*. If they were good, then they made it to the next round, but if they stunk, then they would get the Gong.

After walking around the mall, we went to the auditorium where *The Gong Show* would be. It was right next to

Soul Beat. Soul Beat was Oakland's own TV station and we were proud of it.

"Who do you think is going to win today?" Victor asked.

"We don't even know who is going to perform, fool," James said.

"Yeah bruh, I just want to see somebody get the exit!" I chimed in.

With *The Gong Show,* you never knew who was going to perform and who was going to win. It was rumored that MC Hammer performed here when he was trying to get a record deal. Hammer was an Oaktown legend, too. He started as a bat boy for the Oakland A's and even back then used to dance to entertain the baseball players and fans.

We found our seat in the back of the auditorium and made sure we were in the center of the row. The auditorium was old-school with a paisley design interwoven in the carpet. The seats were in desperate need of repair and had a dark burgundy color tone. This was all we knew, and I loved every minute of it.

Once in his seat, James playfully slapped Scooter on the back of his neck. But he reached around and made it look like Manny did it. "Quit playing, sucka!" Scooter said directly to James to let him know he knew it was him.

"Make me, fool!" James replied. Scooter had to stretch a long way in order to get James back. I caught an elbow in the process.

"Oh, now you done did it!" I said playfully. We all started slap boxing each other while giggling hysterically until the ushers told us to simmer down.

The show was about to start and the ushers were trying to get everybody to their seats. Just then, the MC took the stage and said, "Good evening and welcome to *The Gong Show*, the place where stars are born or laid to rest. Are ya'll ready to have a good time tonight?"

"Yeah!" the crowd roared.

"I can't even hear ya'll. I said are ya'll ready to have a good time tonight?" the MC repeated, trying to get us to explode in excitement.

"YEAH!" the crowd called out, erupting into a frenzy.

"Good. Because we have some great acts tonight that are sure to have you captivated and entertained. And if not, they get the Gong!"

"Woo hoo! Yeah!" the crowd echoed.

"Coming to the stage we have Keisha Baxter. Give her a nice big Gong Show round of applause!"

The crowd went crazy as Keisha walked to the stage. Keisha was heavyset. She had to be close to 300 pounds and wore a shimmery gold dress. She had a dried-out jerry curl. I felt bad for her because judging from her appearance they would boo her. This crowd was merciless and here was this big round woman looking like a disco ball.

"Hi Keisha, where are you from?" the smooth MC asked. He reminded you of Don Cornelius from *Soul Train*.

"West Oakland," Keisha said, getting a mix of cheers and boos from the crowd.

"What are you planning on singing today, Miss Keisha from West Oakland?" the MC asked.

"I am going to sing "Angel" by Anita Baker," Keisha said with confidence. The crowd began to cheer as she did her thing.

"Ooh, ooh, ooh, ooh, ooh, ooh, ooh, ooh

If I could I'd give you the world

Wrap it all around you

Won't be satisfied with just a piece of this heart

My angel, oh, angel

You're my angel, oh, angel

Dreams are dreams, some dreams come true

I found a real dream, baby, when I found you

You're so strong, but tender too

You're my angel, oh, angel

You're my angel, oh, angel"

—"Angel," **Anita Baker**

The crowd went crazy! This woman could sing! I mean really sing. Her voice had been a gift from God. Her skills were probably honed in the church. It had a gospel feel to it. I was ready to boo, but it was undeniable that Keisha meant business and was not there to be humiliated.

The crew was looking dumbfounded because they didn't want to admit that they were moved by such a touching song. Manny finally broke the silence among us by proclaiming, "Big girls really can hold a note." He said that with a devilish smirk on his face. This was probably something he heard his auntie say. We busted up laughing.

When she finished, Keisha got a standing ovation. The crowd was jumping and I loved being a part of it.

"Next we have coming to the stage the Dynamic Duo!" the MC announced.

Two brothers emerged from behind the curtain wearing matching black Adidas sweat suits. They both had on white shell toe Adidas shoes that complemented the white lines on their jacket and sweatpants. They were the definition of fly. The only cats that dressed like this were wannabe rappers and D Boys.

As my crew gawked at their outfits, the MC asked them, "Where ya'll from?"

"We from that 6-5 Vill."

The crowd went crazy because this was their hood after all. They must have been known too because everybody perked up to see their performance.

Oakland had street numbers like many urban cities. If you lived anywhere in the 70th–79th block, we called that the 700 zone, 60th–69th was the 600 zone, and so on. We didn't have Crips and Bloods like in Los Angeles, but we definitely had "Turf Wars." Most disputes were over drugs being sold on someone else's turf, but you could get your head put on flat for talking trash and not being from that zone, or turf. My crew represented 700 because we were all born and raised on 78th. The rap duo was from the 600 zone because of their 65th upbringing. There is no beef unless somebody does something disrespectful.

The 6-5 Village was a housing project. The housing project by my house was 77th Greenside and was small in comparison to the Village. I always heard of people being shot, stabbed, or beat up, walking through the Village, and it was off-limits to me and my crew. The Dynamic Duo had instant street credibility by merely mentioning the 6-5 Vill.

"What are ya'll going to perform?" the MC asked.

"We are going to perform an original called 'Oakland Street Life.' Drop the beat!" they said.

When the music came on blasting, the group began to rap. It looked like one of the cats rhyming forgot his lines and had a blank expression on his face. The crowd picked up on it, and with no remorse, began to BOO. Also, a few "Get the hell off the stage" were thrown in.

Scotty the Clown came out doing a silly shuffling-and-jiving type of dance, spun around to the big Gong, and hit it with a powerful strike. BOOOOOONG! This was the ultimate price to pay for not coming with your best stuff. Scotty did a sweeping motion toward the duo, and they were ushered off the stage. They took it in stride because they knew they were dressed fly and probably had a bunch of cute girlies waiting for them back at the crib.

I looked to the left and several rows ahead I noticed Evelyn and her girlfriends. Evelyn was looking good with her hair neatly plaited in pigtails. Her hair must have just been braided because the lines were perfectly even and not a single hair was out of place. She had on a pair of all-white Reebok Classics and a pink T-shirt that matched the barrettes in her hair. Her tight-fitting blue jean shorts hugged her cute hips and booty.

Her friends didn't even compare to Evelyn. Dee Dee was chunky and had big breasts for her age. Dee Dee had gone through puberty early. She would probably be cute if she lost a little weight. She tried hard to match Evelyn's fly dress habits. My boy Scooter liked Dee Dee.

Michelle dressed ratty and had lots of pimples on her face. Whenever she would start to clown, the fellas would call her "Pizza Face," and that would shut her down quick. Michelle was humble and was the voice of reason in her group. They always listened to her.

Porsche was down to earth, but you could tell she was a gold digger in training. Her mother had champagne taste on a beer budget. That's why her mother named her after a car she could never afford, a Porsche. She was cute with a mouth full of braces. Rumor had it that she had already done it with one of the D Boys from 77th Greenside.

Whenever I saw Evelyn, something moved inside of me. I knew I was going through puberty and my hormones were in full affect. I had a few hairs growing in my private areas and some in my arm pits. I used to want to hit the girls and now I found myself wanting to ask them if they wanted to chill later. How did this happen? What was going on with me? Was

I brave enough to ever say something to her? What if she laughed in my face?

Every summer, we would play boys versus girls, which was really a big game of hide-and-go-seek. The girls would try to find all the boys as a group and then we would try to find them. The older teens played a more advanced version called "Hide and Go Get It."

We alternated between freeze tag, doorbell ditch, and hide-and-seek with the girls. Most times, if it was just the boys, we would play sports like basketball, football, and baseball. The girls would play double dutch, hop scotch, or tetherball at Parker Elementary School.

Although I knew Evelyn and she knew me, I was still afraid to tell her I had a crush on her.

"I see you staring at Evelyn, bruh. She got you sprung," Scooter said to me.

"No I wasn't, fool. I was looking at who was coming on next," I said, trying to play it off.

"Ronald and Evelyn sitting in a tree," sang Scooter. The gang all chimed in too.

"Shut up ya'll! And Scooter you can't talk because you like Dee Dee, blood," I said.

"True, true," James said. Manny threw a skittle in the girls' direction and hit Dee Dee in the back of the head.

"Who did that?" Dee Dee called out. She was looking right in our direction. We all looked in a different direction to make it seem like we were watching the show all along. Evelyn was still facing the stage.

"The next person throw something at me I'm going to get my brother to kick your ass!" Dee Dee said. We believed her because her brother, Darcel, was nobody to play around with.

"Hey Evelyn!" Scooter yelled.

She turned around to face us. "What?"

"My homeboy, Ron, likes you," Scooter said, and he pointed to me. The tips of my ears began to turn a rosy red. I was light skinned enough for you to tell I was blushing.

"Shut up Scooter!" I said, embarrassed.

Evelyn smiled and turned back around to watch the show. What was that smile? She didn't gag? She didn't diss me? Maybe the feeling was mutual? Maybe she just didn't have a response?

"What you do that for?" I said to Scooter, with base in my voice.

"Man, I was just messing with you. Besides, I think she likes you, too. Don't be mad at me, Ronnie."

How could I be mad at this guy? He was the prankster that I always knew Scooter to be. He might have cracked the door open for me to ask if she wanted to hold hands. I was smitten.

It was getting late as we watched the last performers. They were break dancers who went by the name of This N That. These dudes were spinning, popping, and locking. At the end of their set, they all froze in a Break Boy, or B- Boy stance, and the crowd went crazy.

"Eh, I gotta get home," James said.

"Me, too," Manny concurred.

We had the time of our lives. We all walked over to our bikes, feeling entertained, but tired. We didn't have a care in the world. Go to school, do your homework, and clean up after ourselves. While our parents hustled to make ends meet, all we had to do was do well in school. Saturdays like this felt so freeing. Kinda felt like an adult without the responsibilities. I loved my hood. I loved my family. I loved my crew!

The feeling of euphoria eased out of my body as soon as I heard, "Hey Ron, come here, bruh." It was Tyrell. In my mind, I was thinking, I just want to get home. I acted as if I didn't hear him. "Come here for a second," he said, with much more base in his voice.

I got that uneasy feeling I get at the pit of my stomach when I sense danger. My bike crew all rode over to where Tyrell was standing. He had on an all-black T-shirt, sagging blue jeans, and dirty Nike Cortez.

"What's up Tyrell?" I asked nervously.

"Let me borrow your bike real quick. I have to make a run."

"I can't," I said and started to turn to ride toward Hillside.

"C'mon man! I told you I'll be right back," he said as his frustration was starting to build.

Why was he asking me anyway? I wondered. Out of all of my friends, why was he asking *me*? I looked down at their bikes and then again at mine. My bike looked so much better than theirs. It was new and had nice yellow mags on it. I could see why now.

"I can't... I'm sorry," I said, hoping he would finally leave me alone.

"Why not? I'll be right back."

"Because...my mom and dad said I can't let NOOOBODY ride my bike," I replied, trying not to be condescending.

He reached for my handlebars and I pivoted the opposite direction, causing him to miss. I took off on my bike with my boys right behind me and Tyrell running after us.

That was the rule in the hood: Don't let nobody ride your bike or you will never see it again. He would have to take it from me, and I would die for my bike.

Tyrell eventually got tired of chasing. Besides, you can't beat a bike on foot. I'm Audi 5000 to the next day.

Chapter 3

The City of Dope

City of Dope, I call it Oak
Can't be broke, selling coke
Fat ropes, shattered hopes
Fresh cars and all that dope
Baseheads keep the trade alive
Nobody knows about a 9 to 5
Everybody's just trying to survive
You need a gun, can't use those knives
You got a bullet? Well just pull it
And if you trip, get pistol-whipped
By a psycho-maniac sick in his head
Wanna be a gangster, now he's dead
His brother took over, ain't no sweat
Bought a new drop-top white Corvette
Now he's buying keys, making G's
And all the girls say "Won't you please
Take me" in the City of Dope

—"The City of Dope," **Too Short**

My friends and I often went to the store on MacArthur because it was the next closest store. MacArthur was a busy street. It ran from East to West Oakland. Crack was destroying my city. Women who were young and beautiful were now run-down tweakers. Most times you could tell a crackhead by how they dressed and their missing teeth. Men who used to be strong and good- looking came around begging for change until they had saved enough money to buy a rock. Ten dollars was all they needed for a hit. The crackheads would walk from 73rd and MacArthur to 82nd and MacArthur with TVs, VCRs, stereos, microwaves, jewelry, fur coats, sneakers, and whatever they could get their hands on. You could get something that was expensive for twenty bucks.

Manny was always talking about being tired of not having money, and every week I had to remind him how the Dope Boys on our block were always getting locked up. Selling dope was appealing to all of us because it was a way to make a lot of money fast.

Growing up in East Oakland, we noticed the people who made money were street dealers. They seemed to be entrepreneurs who did not answer to anyone. Drug dealing could be attractive to a young mind that has yet to develop the consciousness that drug dealing is helping to destroy black communities.

We looked up to this OG by the name of Todd. We called him Cadillac Todd because he had four Cadillacs—all different colors and different models. Todd would hand out five dollar bills to me and my crew when we got good grades. Todd was the man, but he was always in and out of the joint.

Seeing the way Todd lived his life taught me that all that glitters is not gold.

With a scarcity of black lawyers, educators, engineers, and doctors, and an influx of street pharmacists, a young black boy's mind can get distorted. People learn from one another through observation, imitation, and modeling. Young black teenagers mimicked what was happening in Oaktown in the eighties and early nineties.

As I rode my bike down MacArthur, I looked around at what was happening to my city. I hated seeing so much trash on the ground and people so dependent on drugs. I hated seeing my own black and brown brothas and sistahs in despair.

In front of the liquor store on MacArthur (Mac) were crackheads all surrounding Tremaine, Baron, Blac, and Raymond. They all dropped out of King Estates in the 8th grade to sell dope. Baron was Tyrell's older cousin. Baron didn't want Tyrell to drop out of school like he did to sell dope. Tyrell had already been held back a grade twice, and if he didn't change, he would wind up like Baron, caught in the cycle.

My friends and I would give the dope fiends colorful names because we didn't know their real names and we saw them on Mac all the time. There was Leaning Leon because when he walked he leaned to the side. Drugs had him strung out bad. He looked like the human version of the Leaning Tower of Pisa. Word on the street was he could steal you anything for twenty bucks. That's enough to get a fat rock

Then there was Crackhead Cara, who used to be a prom queen at Oakland High School; now she was a street hooker. Her teeth were so jacked up from years of smoking crack and getting in and out of cars doing Lord knows what.

Last, there was Dave the Dopefiend. I named him Dave the Dopefiend after my favorite Slick Rick song, "Children's Story." "Dave the Dopefiend shooting dope who don't know the meaning of water or soap!" Dopefiend Dave's stench was so bad that you could smell him coming before you seen him.

Speaking of the devil, I think I smelled Dave coming now.

We were riding our bikes past 76th and MacArthur as Dave approached us. "Hey Young Blood, I have a brand-new Spalding Basketball. Give me five bucks for it."

Dave's clothes were ragged and he kept looking over his shoulders like the police was after him. Dave looked sneaky and was always scheming.

All the old heads called us youngsters "Young Blood." Young Blood is a teenager with a lot of energy. They used to say it in the sixties as a term of endearment. All my Oakland peers dropped the "young" and called each other "blood." We take certain phrases and make it our own. Our language flourished with slang and euphemisms. Blood was the bond that we shared with one another, but in Los Angeles, the Crips and Bloods had another meaning. When my mom would take me and my friends to LA, we would stop calling each other "blood" altogether or deal with the consequences.

"I don't have five bucks," I said.

"C'mon blood. I know ya'll have something?" begged Dave the Dopefiend.

"All I have is dollar," James said.

"I have a dollar, too," I said.

"I have two dollars. Give it to us for four bucks, man," said Scooter.

"Okay, okay. Give it to me," Dave the Dopefiend said, with desperation in his voice.

We put our money together and handed it over to him. He was happy to get it and handed the ball over to James. Dave walked off fast right over to Tremain, Baron, Blac, and Raymond. I guess that's all he needed to score a rock.

"That's a brand-new basketball, blood," Manny said.

"Feel the leather. Has to be worth at least thirty dollars, bruh," Victor added.

"We can play ball tomorrow morning before school," I said.

"I love a good dopefiend discount," Scooter said.

"Blood, what did Too Short say in that one song? Oh yeah... 'I come from City of Dope... Probably couldn't be saved by John the Pope!'" We all giggled, but deep down were feelings of helplessness, pity, and anguish.

Chapter 4

King Estates Jr. High School— School Daze

THE POOL PLAYERS.
SEVEN AT THE GOLDEN SHOVEL.

We real cool. We
Left school. We

Lurk late. We
Strike straight. We

Sing sin. We
Thin gin. We

Jazz June. We
Die soon.

—"We Real Cool," **Gwendolyn Brooks**

The weekend was over. Monday had rolled around fast and the crew was off to school. We all met on the corner of 78th Avenue to walk down to 82nd and Hillside to catch the 46 or the 46L with limited stops. The bus came like clockwork and we got on. The 46 bus took us up 82nd Ave. through the curvy turns of Golf Links Road. Then it went up Fontaine Hill. King Estates was on the top of a hill, but was not considered the Oakland Hills. The population didn't reflect the Hills, but a combination of kids on Section 8 and food stamps.

"Wassup ya'll," I said to everybody.

"I sure don't feel like going to school today, but I'm already behind in English and I need to graduate," Scooter said.

"I feel you," chimed in Victor. "I need to get a 70 percent on my Algebra final to pass."

"Let's study after class. I can show you a few things that helped me when I took Algebra," James offered.

"Fareal? Thanks J. But keep it cool. If the older cats hear us or see us talking about studying, they will call us squares and I ain't trying to go through that right now."

Victor was right. If the older homies saw us studying or carrying books, they would pick on us and we would never hear the end of it. It was weird that way in the hood. You almost felt trapped. If you tried hard in school, they would call you a "sucka" or a "mark."

It was easy to thrive at King Estates Junior High School. The students didn't care about doing their homework or getting into a good high school and then college. All they cared about was who had the freshest outfits.

"I'll make sure nobody sees me carrying books to your house, Victor. I don't want to have to throw my books in a pizza box again," James added.

"That was a close call," I said.

We reminisced about the time we were all walking down MacArthur Boulevard and the older homies on the block were posted. Tremaine, Baron, Blac, and Raymond were grinding and selling D in front of the liquor store. They thought that anybody who wasn't hustling were stool pigeons, not thinking about the fact that if you did well in school you could get a good job and potentially make more money with less consequences.

Last year, we were walking to get a salami sandwich from the corner store on MacArthur. They often referred to MacArthur as "Crack Arthur" because of all the crack being sold there. School had just let out and basketball season was over, so we didn't have practice.

"I am starving. Come with me to the store," James said, books in hand.

"It's all good," I replied.

The crew followed as we got off the bus from school on MacArthur and we saw the older cats in front of the store. James was the only one who had his books because the rest of us had left ours in our locker.

"Damn, I see Tremaine and them in front of the store," James said.

"So what!" Manny said, with much bravado.

"So what? They will take my books, rip them up, and toss them in the dumpster if they think I study. I hate them. I really do. Why won't they just leave us alone?" James said.

"Maybe they will be too busy to pay us any attention," I said, not really believing what I just said.

"I am not taking that chance," James said, reaching behind into an open recycling bin and pulling out an empty pizza box. He shoved his Geography, Algebra, and English books inside. He started carrying the box right side up, like there was a hot pizza in there, and had I not seen him put his books in there, I would be none the wiser.

"Oh thanks, bruh. You shouldn't have," Blac said, referring to the pizza box in James's hand.

"Trust me I didn't," James shot back.

James had heart and he wasn't going to back down from no one. Plus, he had to sell the idea that a hot pepperoni pizza was in the box and not books. "This is for my mom and auntie, Blac," James said to Blac. He wasn't pleading with them, but wanted to make sure they thought it wasn't his, so they wouldn't ask for a slice.

Blac had his hands out like James was going to just hand over the pizza. "Come on, little bruh. Your mama ain't going to miss one little slice," he said, trying to convince James.

Blac's teeth and eyes looked so white compared to his jet-black skin. That's why everybody called him Blac. His real name was Antwone. They would joke and say that you needed a flashlight to see him at nighttime.

"Can't do it, man," James said.

"Well, what ya'll doing at the store if ya'll got pizza?" Tremaine said.

"That's his mama and auntie's pizza. We came to get a sandwich. Ya'll been grinding all day. Don't ya'll have hecka money to get your own…?" I asked.

"Shut your nappy head ass up. Ain't nobody even talking to you," Tremaine said. Tremaine was a light-skinned, stocky dude. He had the physique of a running back. Rumor had it that it was from all the weights he lifted when he was in Juvenile Hall.

"I was just telling you," I said, trying to defend myself.

"Give me that box, square!" Blac said.

James slowly started to hand the box over to Blac, and before he could grab it, Baron ran up and yelled, "Five O!"

Blac, Tremaine, Baron, and Raymond ran down 76th. That's what we did in the hood. When somebody yelled "Five O" or "One Time," you better run if you got drugs on you, or you will catch a case if you get caught. I could see them from a distance stuffing their coke bundles behind an abandoned house out of sight of the cops.

"Whew!" James said, as we went in the store.

We got sandwiches and went the other way back home. James still carried the pizza box like he didn't want the cheese to stick to the top. He didn't take his books out until he got in front of his house. It's a shame you can't be a book worm living on your own block. Most kids didn't value education where I'm from and my neighborhood was educationally desolate.

"Yeah, I remember that. That was a close one. You think they would have roughed us up for lying? What do you think would have been worse, lying about having pizza or them finding out we care about school?" I asked.

"Who cares? I'm just glad it's over," James said, with a look of relief on his face.

"See you guys at lunch," Scooter said, and we all went our separate ways.

Between the four of us, we only had a couple of classes together, so I only saw them during lunch and after school. We only had two weeks left in the school year, and I had no one to go to the eighth-grade dinner dance with. The rest of the crew fronted like they had more game than me, but they didn't. We all were virgins. We all were nervous when it came to girls. I had suspected that Scooter had more experience than me. I think he told me he fooled around with a cousin once.

During lunch, we played basketball, but every once in a while, there was a dice game going on behind the school or in the bathroom. The students started shooting quarters, but that was too slow, so they started shooting dollars. Scared money don't make none!

As I walked into the boys' bathroom, I saw about twenty dudes on their knees on the nasty bathroom floor. I should have known that there was a dice game going on because the homie, Quinton, was right in front of the bathroom, keeping a look-out. He let me in because he knew I wasn't a snitch.

Larry was schooling the dice. Schooling the dice was like warming up or getting the dice ready. "Who got me faded?" Larry asked.

"I got you," Scooter said, and put his dollar bill right on top of Larry's. Since we really didn't know Larry all that well, I wanted Scooter to take ALL his loot.

Larry shook the dice and rolled. "Hit him!" he yelled, as the dice rolled a two. Snake eyes on the first roll and you crap out. Two, three, or twelve on the first roll and you crap out. Seven or eleven on the first roll and you hit. Just like rolling dice at the crap table in Vegas.

Scooter picked up the dollar and snatched the dice. "Who got me faded?" he asked, and another kid threw down a dollar on top of his.

Scooter came out of the gate with an eleven and picked up his money. Then he hit again with a seven. Then he rolled a five. I side bet a five to nine and Scooter hit his five after three rolls. He was killing now. He rolled seven again and struck. His next roll was a ten.

"I bet five bucks you don't hit ten," Larry said, feeling anxious because he had lost most of his money and the bell was about to ring.

"Bet," Scooter said and dropped his five ones. Larry put a five-dollar bill on top. It took about ten rolls and Scooter hit, yelling out, "Big Ben does it again!"

Scooter picked up the cash from the point he hit and the side bet and then the bell rang. As we walked to class, I asked him, "How much you hit for?"

"Like twenty-five bucks. I was killing until the bell rang," Scooter said. We saw cats in the hood hit for hundreds and even thousands, but this was good for a thirteen year old. I hated to lose money, but loved seeing one of my boys break up a dice game.

The rest of the day flew by. My last class was math, which was my favorite subject. I was good at it. Mr. Onyeador was my Geometry teacher. He was African and really cared about his students. When my teacher cared, it made me care even more. He is the reason I understand the Pythagorean theorem, quadrilaterals, parallelograms, and obtuse angles.

I was walking to the bus stop after class and saw Evelyn heading the same way. Something came over me, and I said, "Hey Evelyn, can I walk with you?"

"Sure," she said. She had on some dark blue Guess jeans and a blue striped shirt that matched her pants and shoes. Her hair was always on point.

The time was now. I wanted to ask her to go to the dance with me. There was nobody near us to clown if she said no. I have to go for mine. I tried to find the words, but nothing came out.

"I saw you coming out of Mr. Onyeador's room. I know you're good at math. Do you think you can help me with my Geometry homework?" Evelyn asked with this sweet innocent look on her face. She was *so* fine.

I could not believe my ears. She asked me for help with math—me of all people. She left me an opening, too. I wasn't going to blow it this time either.

"Only if you go with me to the dinner dance," I said nervously, waiting on her response.

"I would love to," she replied.

My world could have just frozen in time. I was so happy I felt like skipping all the way to the bus stop. She grabbed one of my notebooks that was on top of my books and wrote her number down on the first page.

"Call me so we can talk about what colors we are going to wear. I think I want to wear this red dress I saw at the mall."

"Oh…okay," I stuttered back. I hadn't even thought that far ahead and she was already planning our colors.

"I got to go meet Dee Dee and them. Call me…K" Evelyn said as she ran off.

My heart was filled with love and I didn't even know what real love was. I was smitten over her. She had made up for all the doubt and nervousness I had ever experienced. Then I felt someone playfully slap me in the back of the head.

Scooter, James, and Victor were standing right behind me. "Did I just see what I thought I saw?" Scooter asked.

"What did you think you saw?" I responded coyly.

"We thought we saw Evelyn giving you the digits, Mack Ron," James said.

"Yeah, she coming with me to the dinner dance," I said proudly.

"That's what I'm talking about, Mack Ron!" the boys said, and they called me Mack Ron all the way home.

Yeah, I was on cloud nine and I didn't plan on coming down soon.

Chapter 5

1989 Battle of the Bay—
A's versus Giants

Buddy, you're a boy, make a big noise
Playing in the street, gonna be a big man someday
You got mud on your face, you big disgrace
Kicking your can all over the place, singin'

We will, we will rock you
We will, we will rock you

Buddy, you're a young man, hard man
Shouting in the street, gonna take on the world someday
You got blood on your face, you big disgrace
Waving your banner all over the place

We will, we will rock you, sing it!
We will, we will rock you, yeah

Buddy, you're an old man, poor man
Pleading with your eyes, gonna get you some peace someday
You got mud on your face, big disgrace
Somebody better put you back into your place, do it!

We will, we will rock you, yeah, yeah, come on
We will, we will rock you, all right, louder!
We will, we will rock you, one more time
We will, we will rock you
Yeah

—"We Will Rock You," **Queen**

Last year, I learned the true meaning of being scared shitless. I was playing football for Arroyo Park's flag football team. I played wide receiver on offense and linebacker on defense.

Arroyo Park is a beautiful park located right off Bancroft. It is a couple of miles long and wide. It hosts two baseball fields, basketball courts, two football fields, a recreation center, picnic areas, and BBQ pits galore.

My friends and I played many sports in Arroyo Park. Oakland Babe Ruth Little League was also held there, but most of my friends and I cut our teeth with Joe Morgan's Tee Ball League when we were five years old.

On the north end of Arroyo Park is a creek that runs the whole length of the upper end of the park. When Victor and I were eight years old, he found an old rusty pistol in the creek. After trying to fire it a couple of times, Victor gave it to the security guard for him to turn in to the police.

You never know what will happen in East Oakland from day to day, hour to hour, or sometimes minute to minute. I was well aware of what lurked in terms of street life, but natural disasters were folklore...right?

I was pissed off because I would be missing Game Three of the World Series. The Oakland Athletics were on their way to sweeping the San Francisco Giants. Even though I was born in San Francisco, I rooted for the Oakland A's all the way.

The Giants had an incredible team led by Will Clarke, Kevin Mitchell, and Matt Williams. They had great pitching and great hitters, but my A's were here to sweep them, so get the brooms ready!

The A's were going to win it all this year with their long list of All Stars, including: Ricky Henderson, Jose Canseco, Mark McGwire, Dave Stewart, and Dennis Eckersley. We had the squad to get it done. And I would miss it because of practice. What could I say? I was a sports addict.

Scooter's dad was our coach and he kept us sharp. He coached us in football and basketball. Coach Tony played football back in the day, and he was a football and track star. I liked going to practice, because after it was over, I could get a ride home, being that I lived across the street from Scooter.

"Man, I can't believe we are missing the World Series, blood," I said to Scooter.

"Yeah, I know, right," Scooter said.

"Maybe if we finish early we can watch the end of it," I said optimistically.

We went through practice running our drills. First, we ran laps around the football field as a warm-up. Coach Tony broke us up into offense and defense groups. Defense practiced rushing the quarterback and the offense practiced running routes.

After we ran all our drills, Coach Tony divided us up into two teams and we had a scrimmage. Scooter and I were on opposite teams. Scooter was a big trash talker, and half the time, I was just trying to keep up.

I was guarding him on defense and he was lined up as a wide receiver. "I'm 'bout to go deep on you, bruh. Consider yourself burnt like toast!" Scooter yelled.

"Not a chance!" I yelled back.

They go deep and Scooter has a step on me, but the ball is thrown too high, allowing me time to catch up and knock the ball out of bounds.

We went back and forth like this for hours. Scooter's team scored a touchdown and went ahead and we caught back up. Eventually, Coach Tony was ready to end practice. Scooter had beaten me yet again, 56 to 49. It was a hard-fought effort, but somebody had to lose, right? There could only be one winner.

"We whipped ya'll…once again," Scooter bragged.

"I would hardly call winning by one touchdown a whipping, but great game."

I was taught to be a good sport when I lost and be humble when I win. Scooter did not care. He loved to gloat. So the bragging began as soon as we left the football field until we walked to the recreation center.

"You can't hold me!" Scooter said.

"You can't hold me… I'm in a league of my own."

"You can't hold me!" he repeated, trying to get a reaction from me.

"You had a good game and your quarterback was David, our starting QB, and we had John John, the practice QB. They are on two different levels," I said.

"Excuses, excuses... Why can't you just admit that I cooked your goose, bruh? You can't hold me," Scooter said, pushing me, with a sly look on his face.

"Shut up!" I said, pushing him back. "Let's get some Gatorade from the snack bar."

The snack bar had all sorts of goodies, from Cup of Noodles to Snickers, Skittles, popcorn, and nachos. It's where we went to replenish if our folks hadn't made dinner yet.

I started thinking about what flavor Gatorade I wanted, and then I felt the ground underneath my feet start to shake violently. The ground was shaking so hard it did not feel real.

Books were falling off the bookshelf. Cats and dogs were outside going crazy. They say animals are great predictors of when something bad was going to take place.

Just then, I heard Ms. Reynolds yell, "Get down!" But all I could make out over all the screaming was "doooown."

I looked down at the floor perplexed. Then a mob of about forty kids were running toward me. Scooter grabbed my arm to indicate that I should follow him under this big wooden table in the front of the rec. center.

That was the protocol when you are faced with an earthquake. Get under a desk or table or stand in a doorway, that way, if anything fell from the ceiling, you would be protected. The table was our best option in this situation.

"Scooter, wait!" I yelled, trying to get him to let go of my arm. I had not had a chance to go to the bathroom since before practice.

Everyone piled under the table like a football scrum. My stomach was bubbling and the ground was shaking out of control. I was terrified and I had two kids on top of me.

Kids kept piling under the table and it seemed it would be impossible to get out of this. Then the unthinkable happened. As I clinched and tried to hold poop from escaping until I made it to the bathroom a little kind of slipped out.

Suddenly, the earthquake stopped. It was finally over. What felt like 10 minutes of uncertainty and chaos was over. Everyone was still. Nobody made a sound.

The silence was broken by Ms. Reynolds saying, "Come up from under the table, everybody."

As the sea of students started to get up from under the table, somebody said, "What's that smell?" I knew he was talking about me, but nobody else did. The earthquake shook the doo doo out of me. I was just that scared. I ran to the bathroom and cleaned myself up good before anyone had noticed.

When I got out of the bathroom, I found Scooter. I knew my parents would be worried sick about me, so I asked Coach Tony to give me a ride home. I must admit that it was super convenient that my best friend's dad was also my coach.

"Thanks Coach Tony," I said. "Peace Scooter. See you tomorrow."

"See you tomorrow, cooked goose," Scooter replied.

I rode my bike as fast as I could home. I ran upstairs to see my mom and dad. I didn't see my mom's car. "Hey Dad, are you all right?" I yelled out.

The power had gone out in the whole neighborhood. I went around and opened all the blinds and curtains so we could have some light. If we had no power when the evening got here, we would light candles. I had seen my mom do it before.

"I'm in the living room," my dad said.

As soon as I walked into the living room, my dad gave me a big hug. He had a tight grip. My father, being from the East Coast by way of Washington, D.C., had never experienced a real earthquake before. We were both shaken up...literally.

My father did not hug me that often. He didn't express himself that way, and when he did, it was because he was really worried about me.

"I'm glad you are all right. Your mother hasn't made it home yet. Help me pick up stuff around the house," he said.

"Okay Dad," I replied, feeling loved.

We walked around the house and put things back in place. Books had fallen off the bookshelf. The mantle above the fireplace was in disarray and needed to be organized. I swept up a broken dish, and after that, we were done.

"Where's Mom? Has she called?" I asked.

"She should be on her way. I pray nothing happened to her," my dad said.

Just then, the power came back on. I heard voices outside, so I looked behind the curtain to see what was going on. Everybody who was on the front porch talking to their neighbor about the quake started going back inside. My block was a community. We all knew each other, and sometimes it was good, but other times folks were all up in your business.

"That was the biggest earthquake we have ever been through," I said, "although last month we had another major earthquake in Oakland, if you can call it that."

"Huey P. Newton, co-founder of the Black Panther Party for Self- Defense, was gunned down and they never found the assailants. I remember you and Mom made me read about the Black Panther Party and how they would organize to make sure we knew our rights. They made sure the police were not racially profiling black folks. They started a breakfast program to feed hundreds of kids throughout the Oakland community and held Saturday school to teach us what we weren't learning in school, like all the black accomplishments and our history, tracing back to Africa," I said.

"Wow son, you remember quite a lot," my dad said, sounding impressed.

"I remember seeing Free Huey graffiti painted on the building walls. I thought he was still in jail?"

"No, he was released, and even though he had his struggles with drugs, he still was one of the most important figures in the movement. Huey P. Newton will be sorely missed," my father said somberly.

"Why do you think that Huey wasn't talked about in the news very much?" I asked.

"Well Ron, the news will cover what they want and leave out certain things to appease the mainstream viewers. It's called media propaganda. I will teach you more about that sometime. Let's watch the news and see what kind of damage this earthquake caused."

I sat next to him on the couch in the living room as he turned the channel to KTVU Channel 2 news.

More than fifty dead and hundreds injured in what was being called the Loma Prieta earthquake. Later, folks would refer to it as the World Series earthquake or the '89 quake.

Part of the Nimitz freeway collapsed in West Oakland. My dad called the freeway 880. When the news reporter said that part of the Bay Bridge had collapsed, I couldn't believe it.

My mother worked at James Lick Middle School in San Francisco. She was the librarian. She crossed the Bay Bridge every day. My eyes began to fill with water.

"What's wrong?" my dad asked.

"What if..." I started, but stopped, when I heard the front door handle turn. It was my mom and my sister. I ran over to my mom and jumped into her arms. I hugged my sister Leah, who didn't really seem to know what was going on.

"I love you, Mom. I'm glad you made it home."

"Aww, I love you, too."

"Love you, Mom. Love you, Ronnie," Leah said.

"Love you, too, sis."

Leah looked like she just woke up from taking a nap in the car. I told my mom about everything on the news. I explained to her that had she left an hour later she would be a goner.

The World Series earthquake had caused the biggest baseball game of the year to be postponed ten days—not to mention all the landslides and the walls and buildings that collapsed. Rubble fell to the ground and fires had started, thanks to the earthquake.

I looked up at my mom one last time before going to bed and whispered, "I'm so glad you made it, Mom, because I don't know if I could survive just being with Dad."

We both laughed and hugged and then headed for bed.

Chapter 6

Black Boy Lost

They won't let me get a phone call, but they better

Not let me write a letter

I wrote the Uhuru House and told them

To bring the helicopter to the courtyard and drop the
rope

And I'll be right there

With my Black Power Fist soaring high in the air!

— *"Ward of the State,"* **Askari X**

I was a thirteen-year-old black boy discovering the meaning of what it is to be black in America. I wore my culture on my sleeve and there was no escaping. In the news, my life was not worth air time. People were getting shot in my hood every day, but we didn't hear about it. If someone was shot in Montclair, Piedmont, the Oakland Hills, or any other rich area near Oakland, then it made the front page. Go figure.

"Yo, come with me to the store, bruh," I said to Scooter. But he was too busy playing his Walkman to pay me any attention.

I elbow-tapped him to get his attention, and he took the headphones from his ears. "What's up, man?" he said.

"Come with me to the store," I said again.

"Okay."

We made our way down the street, just letting the bike glide. I felt the breeze against my face as we cruised past all the houses on our street. Growing up in the hood, you are never far away from a liquor store.

Scooter and I leaned our bikes against the wall and strutted into the store. I was just happy that I had some change in my pocket. I still had a couple of bucks from when I helped my dad cut the backyard lawn.

When I walked in the store, I noticed Arab Arash wasn't there, and in his place was some new guy I never saw working that shift before. It made no difference as long as he could give me back my change.

I was thirsty, so I went to the back of the store, where I knew they kept pineapple Crush, which was my favorite soda. "You want a soda?" I asked Scooter.

"Yeah. Get me an orange one," Scooter replied.

"I got you."

I opened the door to the soda refrigerator and grabbed one pineapple and one orange one. I didn't have a good grip on the soda in my left hand because it was so cold and a little damp from the moisture on the outside of the can. It slipped completely out of my hand and made a thud when it hit the ground. It sounded louder because of the quietness in the store.

Scooter walked around the aisle just in time to see me drop the soda. "BUTTER FINGERS!" he yelled. "Ha, ha, ha!" Scooter was cracking up.

I grabbed the soda off the ground and turned toward the counter and noticed the clerk had a gun pointed at me and Scooter.

We froze because we both knew that any sudden move and this nervous racist dude would blow our heads off. I wished I could say that this is my first time seeing a gun, but every New Year's Eve all the D Boys would fire guns into the air. I could even tell the difference between certain hand guns.

"You damn thugs are always in here stealing and I'm sick of it," said the clerk. He was a young man who couldn't be over the age of twenty-five. He had never worked in a neighborhood like this. Obviously, he was mistaking us for someone else. He was of Middle-Eastern descent, possibly related to Arab Arash.

"Look man, I am going to pay for this. I have money. Put the gun down. We come here all the time," I said, pleading with the man.

"SHUT UP! SHUT UP!" the clerk said.

"Hey man, PLEASE DON'T SHOOT. We're sorry," Scooter said, while we both still had our hands in the air. Scooter was apologizing for absolutely nothing at all.

"SHUT UP! I'm calling the cops!"

"We have money to pay. We don't have anything in our pockets but the money we came in with," I said to the clerk, trying to rationalize with him.

The clerk looked as if he was thinking over what to say or do next. I knew some of the boys in this neighborhood do come in this store just to shoplift but that wasn't us. I and Scooter were always in fear of that butt whipping our moms and pops would put on us. We knew that stealing a soda or a ten-cent pack of candy was not worth the leather welts on our legs, butt, and back. To this clerk, we were just some dirty little black kids with no morals, values, or home training. He saw us as D Boys in the making, getting ready for the penitentiary.

"We will never come back; just don't shoot," Scooter said, begging for our lives.

The clerk kept the gun pointed directly at us. He never lowered his gaze and looked like he was a trained assassin. His face was a mix of hatred and insecurity. "GET OUT AND DON'T COME BACK!" he screamed, motioning to the door with the pistol.

What felt like eternity was probably only one minute. We wasted no time making an exit. Scooter and I were both sweating and at a loss for words. We didn't get on the bikes, but instead walked on the side of them, as if we had a flat tire. Our minds wondered. Not quite sure what to make of what just happened.

To that clerk, my life wasn't worth a damn. All he knew was what the TV shows. Black boys rob. Black boys steal. Black boys sell dope. Black boys have no respect. Black boys are thugs.

Our neighborhood didn't make things better because there were actually black boys who did those things. Some of them felt like there was no other way to make money. When you are faced with the deck stacked against you, it forces you to make something out of nothing.

Scooter and I didn't talk for several minutes. We were just trying to figure out what to say. Scooter's house was fast approaching. We get to his house and lay our bikes down. I turned to face Scooter and saw his eyes watering. Scooter was one of the hardest boys I knew, and just the mere fact of what just transpired was too much for both of us to handle.

"You want to talk about it?" I asked, trying to break the silence.

"Nah," Scooter replied, sounding as if he had a frog stuck in his throat.

Tears started flowing from both of our eyes at the same time. I was sobbing and trying to catch my breath. If anybody in the hood would have seen us, we would have lost ALL credibility. But we didn't care.

The streets didn't love us. The only person that would show me love was my mom. My dad was always taking out his life stressors on me. Hell, he didn't have time to show love. I guess we were just two black dudes trying to deal with the pressure of being African in America.

Scooter came closer to give me a hug and I let him. We embraced as if we had not seen each other in years. One of those long heartfelt hugs that you give someone when they tell you they just lost a relative. Our T-shirts were wet on the top because we had been standing there crying for well over 5 minutes, but I didn't care. I had to get it out and formulate what I would do next.

"I can't believe that sucka pulled a strap on us like we were nothing... less than nothing," I said.

"I ain't ever going back, even if Arash is behind the register," Scooter said as he pumped his fist.

"Me either," I agreed.

"I'm going to tell the crew tomorrow what went down," Scooter said.

"I should tell the big homies to shoot up the corner store," I said, not really thinking it through. What if there were kids in there? That was what was expected of us, but I didn't care at this point, because I was pissed. As I wiped away snot bubbles and tears, I noticed it was getting late.

I give Scooter another hug and told him, "This whole night is my fault. Had I not talked you into going into the store with me, you would not have been there to get a gun pulled on you."

"I almost died today because of you!" Scooter said as a half-smile started to form on his face.

"Shut up, fool. I'm serious," I said to Scooter, who had a way of making light of a situation.

"If that scared dude didn't pull a gun on us, it would have been some other black kids, and he might have used it too," Scooter said.

We both knew that is was a cardinal sin to pull a gun on someone and not use it. The retaliation could be ten times worse. You could lose your crew and family trying to be a tough guy in East Oakland. There were no consequences for this guy to pay. If the police rolled up on him, he could just say he felt threatened.

"You're right, Scoot. We didn't punk out either, although maybe a little..." We both laughed. "You telling your folks?" I then asked.

"I don't know yet, cuz. I'm out. See you tomorrow," he said a second time.

"See you later, cuz," I said and left his porch to head to mine.

Thoughts were swirling in my head about if I should tell my mom and dad what just went down or if I should just let it go. But what if it happens to another black boy? What if I could stop it from happening to another black boy?

When I entered my house, my mom and dad were in the living room, watching *A Different World*. As I watched the show, I thought, when I get older, I am going to an all-black college (HBCU) like Hillman. I looked around and didn't see my sister Leah, so I thought she must be asleep.

"What's up, big guy? How was your day?" my dad asked. He was smiling from watching the comedy and did not see my face.

"What's the matter, baby?" my mother asked. She could always tell when something was up with her only son.

"Nothing, Ma... I'm going to wash up and head to bed, if that's all right."

"Well, give your momma a hug first, and why your eyes so red?" she probed.

As if my mother could summon the truth out of me, my eyes started to water again and I let everything out. I told my folks about the incident at the liquor store.

My father was fuming. Pacing back and forth, he was trying to decide whether or not to go to the store himself or call the police.

"That man put a gun in the face of a thirteen year old, huh? He got to pay!" my dad said, trying not to curse in front of me.

"Calm down, Ronald Senior," my mother said to my dad, being mindful to look right at him, because I am named after him, and it could be confusing when we are all in the room talking together.

"Calm down?" my dad yelled. Leah woke up and came in the room. My dad and mom started arguing back and forth. I just had a traumatic experience and they were here yelling at each other. I took Leah outside to the front porch to play with Legos so she didn't have to hear all the yelling and cursing. We went back in after they stopped yelling. This was a regular occurrence in the Anderson house.

"We will call the police and leave a report. I heard the Uhuru House helps people with discrimination and racist incidents," Mom said.

"But Mom, won't that make me look like a snitch? I don't want to wear the snitch jacket through the hood," I said, a little disappointed.

In East Oakland, everything is based on your reputation. If you are perceived as a snitch, then people would be less likely to associate with you. You were no longer cool. You were no longer down for the set. You were no longer considered part of the block. I didn't want that. This wasn't the type of revenge I was expecting. I didn't want to tattle tale on the guy. What I wanted was my father to whip his ass!

"You won't look like a snitch. You will look like somebody who stood up for himself," my father explained.

It didn't matter what I thought, because my parents were going to do whatever they thought was right, and I agreed most times, but this time, I wasn't so sure.

I did a police report over the phone, because I was not injured or anything, so they didn't have to show up at our house. Thank God, because my nosey neighbors were always in somebody else's Kool-Aid.

The next morning, my dad, Scooter, and I went to the Uhuru House. Scooter got the okay from his parents to go and give his testimony.

The Uhuru House was a community organization that promoted Africa on an international level. *Uhuru* is Swahili for "freedom." They believed in uplifting the people and the community. Uhuru House was formed shortly after the Black Panthers' plight. They had their own community garden and gave food to those in need. In addition, they sold furniture to single parents at a discount. Uhuru House's main focus was social justice for Pan Africans.

When we entered, we were greeted by a couple with long, thick dreadlocks that ran all the way down their backs. I could smell Nag Champa incense burning—I always loved that smell. Portraits of Haile Selassie, Langston Hughes, Paul Robeson, Malcolm X, Bob Marley, Marcus Garvey, Madam C.J. Walker, Kwame Nkrumah, Sojourner Truth, and of course, all the Black Panthers lined the walls.

This was the East Oakland Black Mecca. If you wanted to get in touch with who you are as an African living in North America, then this was the place to be.

Scooter and I told our stories to the couple that ran the Uhuru House. They told us they would talk to the store owners to ensure that this would not happen again. Scooter and I were told to stay away from the store from now on. It was no big deal to us. This was East Oakland, and I am loathe to say that we had hundreds of liquor stores to choose from.

A week later, the weekend rolled around, and I happened to ride by the liquor store, even though I was told not to go in. I saw a group of about twenty people in front with signs. Some signs said "BOYCOTT." Other signs said, "NO JUSTICE, NO PEACE!" It was the Uhuru House! I was happy to see them in action.

I rushed home to ask my mom and dad about the protest and how it started. "Did ya'll know about this?" I asked excitedly.

"Yep," my dad said. "The owner's nephew said he felt threatened. 'Then you don't need to be selling your stuff in our community if you feel threatened by the community you are serving,' they said."

"Power to the people!" I called out. I heard that from a Black Panthers documentary my folks made me watch.

"Power to the people," my father said back. He smiled and gave me dap.

The people who work in our neighborhood are not always from our neighborhood. They are here to make a profit. They don't understand black people or appreciate our rich culture and contributions. How does a black boy navigate this uncaring world? I was thinking. How do I find myself and still be true to these streets? Am I a black boy lost in this unforgiving world?

"Life is to be lived, not controlled;

and humanity is won by continuing

to play in the face of certain defeat."

—*Invisible Man,* **Ralph Ellison**

Chapter 7

The Bus Ride–Riding through the Town

1983 was when I stepped in the game
Back then it was only about twelve known gangs
And I could name them all, nigga on the real
6-9, Stone City, 11-5, 23rd, Sunnyside and Brook-
Field, can't forget the High Street Bank Boys
8-5, Plymouth Rock, Seminary making much noise
Acorns, Bushrod, putting in work
These are real O-G turfs straight from the dirt
Shit done changed, it's 1994
And niggas claimin' shit that I never heard of before
New booty niggas from these unknown places
Ain't from the days of World Cups and Ben Davises
And derbies with your name on the back and Pirate
hats
With a gang of stars and Falcon cars
You new age hustlers, fake-ass player haters
What about the days at the 4-star theater on a
Sunday, or Foothill Square?
You probably never knew it was a skatin' rink there
Niggas wore they belt buckles to the back
5-0-1s saggin', twenty deep on beach cruisers going to
the East Bay Dragons
On a Friday, to get into the mix
Niggas was too young so them E-B-Ds wasn't havin'
it

Fuck it, ridin' down East 1-4, smoking on a tailor
finna go to Mo-
jo's and you can catch hoes throwing blows from
every angle
That East Side Killa crew and them 6-9 Angels
The days of the real livin' by the rules
Just a little somethin' for my peoples from the old
school

—"Old School," **Seagram**

Now don't get me wrong, I like riding my bike more than anything in the world, but when the crew got a chance to get on the bus, that was always something special, whether it was having a full-out cap session ragging on each other's mamas or people watching, but most of the time, we were trying to stay out of turf war zones.

"Last summer, we got blasted on by the girls," I reminded Manny, Victor, Scooter, and James.

"What are you talking about?" said Victor.

"What am I talking about?" I said, mocking Victor. "Last year, after the block party, we lost the water fight because we ran out of supplies. This summer, we get revenge. This summer, we come fully stocked. We need water balloons, and has anybody seen the commercial for the Super Soakers?" I asked.

The Super Soaker looked like what water guns are supposed to be. I never seen a gun hold so much water. Water balloons are hit or miss. I mean sometimes those things don't even explode. What's up with that?

"The only place that is going to have the Super Soakers is going to be at Bayfair Mall in San Leandro," Scooter said.

"I'm not riding my bike all the way to San Leandro and back. Plus, we got hoop practice tomorrow," James said.

James was the wise owl of the crew. He was also the oldest. James was also a triple threat. He was good at sports, good in the books, and the girls liked him. Since he was older, we would listen to James. James was the type of kid your parents would always compare you to. They would say:

"Why can't you be more like James?

I don't think James would have talked back to that teacher.

I don't think James would have used bad words.

I don't think James would have gotten into that fight.

Why can't you be more like James?

James, James, James."

"I see AC!" I said sarcastically, mocking the commercial.

"You see what?" asked Victor, James, and Manny. The only one I didn't fool was Scooter because he saw the commercial when he was at my house.

"I see AC Transit," Scooter said, as he rolled his eyes. We all agreed that it was a stupid slogan.

AC Transit was our bus line and the only thing we knew. It allowed us to go to all the neighboring cities like San Leandro, Alameda, Berkeley, Richmond, and Hayward. AC stood for Alameda–Contra Costa (it should be ACC Transit). We lived in Alameda County, but the bus lines also connected to Contra Costa County with cities like Richmond, El

Sobrante, Walnut Creek, Pittsburg, and so on. But we usually didn't go that far. Not yet at least.

"I don't know about that. I don't think I have fifty cents to get on the bus," Victor said. Money was tight in his family because his dad was the only one working.

"Ron, give Victor a quarter, so we can bounce," Scooter said.

"Why I gotta give him a quarter?" I asked.

"Because you got it," Scooter said, getting irritated. Why did they always assume I had money to give away? Like I have extra money? Okay, sure we did have the biggest house on the block, but this was 78th Ave. I'm not the Fresh Prince and this ain't Bel Air.

"All right, then fine," I said to Scooter defiantly. Scooter knew me. Scooter knew that I did not like to leave friends behind, even if they didn't return the favor. It just didn't feel right.

Begrudgingly, I reached into my pocket, gave Victor a quarter, and said, "Let's walk to the bus stop."

No bikes today because we were all on a mission to catch the 40 bus to Bayfair Mall. I loved walking down Hillside to the bus stop. We were all practical jokers constantly playing around or trying to annoy one another. If someone was behind you, then you had to be aware of a foot trying to trip you.

We made it to the bus stop in no time. Another 6 minutes passed before the 40 bus came. We went straight to the back of the bus because there was always more room and we were free from adults to talk how we wanted. We took over the back of the bus.

My folks were always teaching me about Black History. They were giving me the facts every day of my life. I did not value it at the time, but it gave me a frame of reference. Like how black teenagers get on a bus and automatically go to the back of the bus, forgetting everything that Rosa Parks fought for. Why didn't we sit in the front of the bus as a sign of progress and solidarity?

Do you think these young black boys and girls didn't know their history? Maybe we just didn't care. Being in the back of the bus made us feel free. We could curse and act a fool and nobody would do anything about it. We did not realize what our ancestors had fought for during the civil rights movement and how the bus boycott was the catalyst for the change that took place.

"I need a marker," said Manny.

"What do you need a marker for?" asked James.

"I'm going to mark our set on the back of the bus," Manny replied.

On the back of the bus was a bunch of neighborhoods all over Oakland. I saw West Oakland represented with Acorn, Cypress Village, and the Lower Bottoms. East Oakland was all over the bus. We called this tagging and it was illegal. You could go to Juvenile Hall for tagging, but that didn't stop most youngsters from doing it.

Since the 40 bus went through East Oakland, most of the tags were hoods in East Oakland, everywhere from the Rolling 20's, Dirty Thirties, and Funktown to 65th and 69th Village, 98th and Brookfield, and Shady 80's.

"See. I don't see 700 on here!" Manny said, with more base in his voice.

"Here...look," Victor said.

In the lower corner, someone wrote, "77th Greenside."

"You don't need no marker after all, Manny," James said. "Besides, I am not trying to get in trouble today," he added.

"Word!" Scooter said, as we put to rest Manny wanting a marker to do his tagging.

"What are you trying to be, from New York, son? You want to be the best graffiti artist, kid?" he said, with a New York accent.

"Word is bond, kid," mocked James.

"Yo mad shorties are gonna be at Bayfair, yo'," added Victor. His East Coast accent was on point.

"Yo B. Why you letting shorty over here play you, son?" said Scooter, joining in on the fun.

We talked with our fake East Coast accents until we approached Bayfair. Even though Manny was the butt of the joke, he eventually joined in. If you can't beat us, join us, and it was too fun to resist.

We excitedly hopped off the bus in front of Dunkin' Doughnuts and crossed the street to Macy's. I hated walking through the mall when I didn't have any real money to spend. I had just enough money to get my water balloons, though.

The crew and I cut through Macy's and looked at all the expensive clothing that we couldn't afford. I saw Guess jeans and some overalls at $85 a pair. Then we passed Karl Kani and the Polo section. But when we got to the Cross Colours section we all stopped simultaneously. Cross Colours was loud and definitely hip-hop, with bright reds, yellows, blues, and greens.

Maybe I could ask my mom for some Cross Colours overalls for my birthday since all she said we could afford was Wrangler jeans, unless it was a special occasion. I considered my birthday a special occasion. Besides, they rocked Cross Colours on *In Living Color, Fresh Prince,* and *Martin,* all my favorite TV shows.

The crew marveled at the Cross Colours section, and everybody was talking about which shirt and pants they would sport. We were window shoppers, not intending to buy any of the stuff we were touching and looking at. The lady working that section of Macy's didn't even acknowledge us. I guess she figured that none of us had the cheese to buy anything from there, being dressed the way we were.

"I can't wait to get a job so I can get fly like Martin Lawrence," Scooter said.

"Damn Gina!" Manny said, and the crew busted out laughing.

"Let's go to K&B Toys store so I can get some water balloons," I said.

Everybody left Macy's and we walked around the mall, checking out all the stores and claiming that when we got older, we would have this and that. You have to fake it till you make it.

K&B Toys store was jam-packed with parents and kids shopping. Well, the parents were shopping and the kids were begging for things.

"Here they are!" Victor shouted.

"Oh, you found them," I said to Victor.

"They have different colors, too," James said.

"Let's get red and blue water balloons. Whatever team you're on, that would be your color," Scooter said.

"I like that idea," I said.

We grabbed two bags of each color and walked over to the water gun section. They have the Super Soakers in different sizes from jumbo to smaller.

"I'm going to get one of these on my birthday next month," James stated.

"I wish. It's too much for a water gun. I can hear my dad's voice now. *Mi hijo,* twenty dollars for a water gun. Yo *nunca* ('never')," Victor said.

He was right. We would have to be getting really good grades to even think about getting an expensive toy like the Super Soaker or wait until Christmas or your birthday.

We went over to the line to buy the water balloons. Everybody pitched in, except Victor, because he didn't have no *dinero.*

Right as we were exiting K&B Toys store, a loud alarm sounded.

"What the…" we all muttered in unison.

"RUN!" Manny yelled.

We tore to the emergency exit by the food court and ran as fast as we could through the parking lot. A security guard attempted to chase us, but was too fat and out of shape to keep up.

Several people either just getting to Bayfair or getting in their cars to leave started pointing in our direction.

"Why are we running?!" I yelled, while trying to catch my breath.

"Just run, fool!" Manny said.

With a great stroke of luck, the 40 bus heading back to our hood was slowing down at the bus stop. We waved frantically for the bus driver to see us and he did. We all pulled out our transfers, hopped on the bus, and headed straight to the back of the bus.

"Why in the hell are we running like we stole something?" I asked.

"Because we did," Manny replied.

He reached in the back of his pants and pulled out a Super Soaker. How he was able to run and keep it in his jeans, I will never know.

"Are you crazy?! You could have gotten us ALL in trouble. What's your problem, Manny?" James yelled.

"Yeah!" the rest of us chimed in.

"Dude...that was hella selfish!" Scooter said.

"So you mean to tell me that ya'll don't want to use the Super Soaker?" Manny asked, as if he just won the argument.

"That's not the point. If you want to go to Juvenile Hall, then that's on you, but don't be bringing us into your schemes and plots," I said. "You know how my dad be trippin'. Hell, I can't tell if he loves me or hates me. He's present, but I still feel alone. I told you I am already on thin ice because of the—"

"You all got it made!" Manny said, cutting me off. "My momma don't give me shit! Sometimes I come home and we have no power and no lights on. You ever had to look for a candle and matches in the dark? Huh? Sometimes the water is off and the only way for me to take a good shower is at school after P.E. So if I am out and I want something, I take it. I gotta make it happen because nobody is going to do for me like I do for myself," Manny said.

"Manny, we understand that it is a struggle every day, but none of us here were born with a silver spoon in our mouths," James said.

"You know *mi padre* is the only one working, but you don't see me shoplifting," Victor added.

"Well you should! A little five finger freebie never hurt nobody. K&B Toys makes millions every year. They won't miss it," Manny replied.

"Look dude, if you are going to be stealing and not tell us beforehand, then we can't kick it with you. I'm not trying to go to Juvie," James said.

"Me either," the rest of us said.

"I guess it is what it is. Ya'll ain't got to fool with me no more," Manny said.

The bus ride home was quiet. Nobody said a word. I wanted to see the Super Soaker, but I didn't want Manny to think that what he did was cool. My folks were always telling me about being guilty by association. I could hear them now:

"Be careful who you hang out with. They could bring you down. If one of you gets into a fight and beats up somebody, you all will get in trouble. If one of you guys steal a car and you're in the car, then you all go down. If one of ya'll steals, then you all go to jail. These police out here love locking little black boys up. Don't make a mistake that can ruin the rest of your life," my dad would say.

My mother would be right there as my father preached, hanging on his every word and agreeing, saying, "Um hmm and yes" whenever my dad made a strong point.

I had to start being more careful about who I hang out with because I cared about my life and my future. Manny didn't care about us. He was all for self. That's what he was taught. No respect for others. So why should I have respect for him?

I had to get up early for school tomorrow. I had to take school serious if I wanted to make something of myself.

Chapter 8

A Black Cadaver

Chorus:
Up early in the morn AK Spray Another day another
dead in the Alley way
Up early in the morn AK Spray Another day another
dead in the Alley way
Another day—another dollar—another dead—
another snitch
And a empty clip gottem' laid out expired in a ditch
Letting off 15 shots from my Glock
and got two left up for my patna and another for my
damn self
If push ever came to shove
Out in Oakland, California, where the brothas show
NO LOVE
Wouldn't hesitate or think twice to straight smoke ya
Plant it straight in your membrane. Is part of that
Village culture
From Sun up to Sun down—Brothas found face-
down
Now I'm short a whole clip after my fully spits
rounds
Up early in the morn AK Spray Another day another
dead in the Alley way
Up early in the morn AK Spray Another day another
dead in the Alley way

—"Alleyway," **The Delinquents (featuring The Luniz)**

The next day, I woke up to get ready for school. I had laid out my school clothes the night before. I was going to wear my Georgetown Hoyas T-shirt, blue jeans, and blue Nike Cortez. I waited at the end of 78th and Hillside, where we always met to walk to the bus stop. Today felt different. I was the first one to the corner and gradually James showed.

"What's good, James?"

"Nothing much, man. Only a week and half left in school. Just counting down the days until summer. Yesterday at the mall was crazy."

"*Buenos dias,*" Victor said.

"*Buenos dias,*" James and I said back with our limited Spanish.

"Remember what we were talking about yesterday leaving the mall?" I asked.

"That was some selfish shit Manny pulled this weekend. I'm going to talk to him today," James said.

Finally, Scooter showed up. It took us about 10 minutes to walk down Hillside, and our bus would be arriving in 15 minutes.

"Anybody seen Manny?" Scooter asked.

"Nope," said Victor.

"Not since he stole that water gun from the mall," Scooter said and laughed.

"Well, the bus is coming and we always start walking at 7:45 a.m. If he's not here in 5 minutes, we gotta go," I said.

We waited five more minutes and still no sign of Manny, so we walked down Hillside to the bus stop. The bus made its way up 82nd. It was filled with most of our classmates from the 800 block. The 46 bus picked up those students first because that is the direction it went.

We usually joked on the way to school, but today was different. We were all wondering about Manny. Was Manny really that mad at us that he would miss the rest of school? I know Manny didn't like school, but I thought he understood how important it was to his future.

"Hey, do you think Manny is mad at us?" I asked.

"Mad at *us*? We should be mad at *him*," James said.

"Yeah, at least that fool could have given us the heads-up," Victor said.

"You would think he would show up since we have less than two weeks of school left. I'm mad at him, but still want him to graduate," I said, trying to be the voice of reason.

The wheels of the bus screeched as we made our way up 82nd Ave. to Golf Links Road. Golf Links Road was beautiful with trees, green grass, and a creek. Live oak trees and a few redwood trees make Golf Links Road look like a camping backdrop rather than a neighborhood.

When we were about the size of a football field away from the front of King Estates Junior High School, I saw a large group of people standing in front.

"I wonder what's going on down there," I said.

"Probably a fight," Victor said.

The bus inched closer to the school and we could see that there was a section of bushes that had been enclosed with yellow tape. The bus driver pulled in front of the school and waited for directions from the police.

There were cop cars all around us, and an Asian man with too much gel in his hair walked up to the bus driver's window and told him there was a homicide last night, but you could let the students off the bus now. Everything is okay.

But it wasn't.

All of the students filed off the bus, one by one. I couldn't believe what I saw when I got off the bus. There was yellow tape and around ten police officers pacing back and forth behind the yellow tape. Behind the yellow tape was a black man on the ground covered up by a blanket. Although the blanket covered his body, you could still see part of his legs and feet.

I tried not to look when I walked down the sidewalk in front of the school. I knew I could never work as a homicide detective or in forensics because I hated looking at dead people. I hated the sight of blood.

All of us King students were looking at this deceased black guy as if he was on display at a museum.

Later, we would learn that it was a "drug deal gone bad." This is when a drug dealer and the drug buyer could not reach an agreement or the money was short or any number of reasons to make gunfire take place.

Apparently, this dead man in the bushes was involved in a drug deal and something did not go as planned. My school was just acting as if it was business as usual. There was no school closure. The school officials did not try to shield our innocent eyes from the homicide.

I went from class to class, thinking about what I saw. I had never seen a dead body, except at funerals. I had been to three funerals, and they were all older family members. I had decided I would shake it off and not let it bother me.

The more I tried to shake it off, the more I thought about seeing the dead naked man lying on the ground, with his eyes open, staring into the sky. His expression said, why me? I wondered, were his circumstances so bleak that he had to deal drugs? Did he feel helpless like Manny? Did he feel like this was his last resort?

I thought about all the times me and my friends had looked up to people in our neighborhood who were really getting money. We didn't have doctors, engineers, computer scientists, or lawyers to look up to. The people in our neighborhood who were making money were selling crack. If making some quick money leads to being dropped off, dead, in front of a school, then I didn't want it.

During lunchtime, we played basketball to try to get a sense of normalcy. I had to ask my crew of friends if they were still thinking about this morning like I was.

"Yeah man. I can't stop thinking about it," Scooter said.

"Me either. I mean I've seen a dead body before, but not right after someone has been killed. It's given me the chills," I admitted.

"People are getting blasted in our neighborhood all the time. Why is this morning bothering you? You didn't even know the dude," James said.

"I don't know. It's just spooky to know that probably yesterday at this time that guy was alive. He had a family and friends and now someone killed him and dropped his cold stiff body in the bushes in front of our school," I said.

"That's the rules of the game. If you are going to sell dope, then you have to be ready for what comes with it," James said.

"I guess you are right. But that was cold. They didn't have to do him like that, though."

School let out and Manny never came. He picked a good day to miss.

Chapter 9

Extra Manish

I'm a little manish mutha#$*%

I take after my older brother

Started off selling marijuana but now I'm selling yola

Shit was gettin' hella funky at first

when a nigga was snatchin' a bitch's purse

Ended up gettin' kicked out of every school in Vallejo

they clowned me like a circus

I was the little mannish mother#@% showing out in
the back of the church

My momma was quick to hit me with a switch and I
say "that hurts"

Get to the house, go to my room and talk some trash

I never believed a hard head made a soft ass

Cause I be moving fast and I'd be trying to stash

Beat up the pizza man and then I straight dashed

Disobedient sport cut my days short

My momma got tired of takin' my ass back and forth
to court

I said "Momma I'ma straighten up for you and I
promise I won't front"

Got me a job as a paperboy

21 dollars a month

5 o'clock in the morning

Damn I'm slavin' for the f'ing white man

21 dollars might buy me some porage call me Chicken
George

I'm tired of mutha@%$ f'ing over me

How can I find a way to make some real money?

But you don't feel me

I was tired of being broke lookin' tore down

Came up off a twenty dollar break me down

—"Extra Manish," **E-40**

W e hadn't seen Manny in school all week, and I knew we had that argument, but I was worried about my friend. I walked over to his house and knocked on the door. Manny lived in a gray and blue duplex on the corner of 78th and Hillside. It was a nice-looking apartment that just needed some love.

Nobody came to the door in a couple of minutes, so I knocked again, but louder this time. "Boy, you knocking like the damn police!" Ms. Lewis said.

Ms. Lewis did not look like she could be a mother. She had Manny when she was sixteen, and she still looked young. She had a dark skin complexion and dressed scantily. My hormones were already raging as a thirteen year old and she came to the door in a wife beater, no bra, and boy shorts. Damn yo' mama fine, Manny, was all I was thinking.

"Um, hi Ms. Lewis, is Manny here?" I asked, trying not to stare at her hard nipples poking through the white wife beater.

"No, I thought he would be with you and the rest of ya'll little gang. All I know is that boy better have gone to school," she said, sounding exasperated.

Manny's dad was a mid-level drug dealer who was shot and killed. Manny was only five when it happened, so he never got a chance to know his dad. His father was too busy running the streets to spend any real time with him. When Manny's dad passed away, that left Manny to be the man of the house and tend to his two sisters and one younger brother.

Drug dealers got shot all the time where we lived, so it was no big deal. If you wanted a quick one-way ticket to see your maker, then start selling dope. You could die by the hands of a junkie trying to steal your dope bundle. You could die by a rival from another turf that wanted your territory. You could die from a jealous member of your own team. You could die by the racist cops that shoot first and ask questions later.

"Can you tell him I came by? Thanks," I said and hopped back on my bike and cruised down the street. I would swing by Arroyo Park to see if he was there playing football.

I was on a solo mission today to find my friend. I liked being with the crew, but I also liked being alone sometimes. I could get more accomplished by myself and didn't have to wait for a collective decision to be made on what to do next.

I did not see Manny at the park and was starting to worry because he wasn't at school all week. I felt my stomach starting to churn because I hadn't eaten since lunch. My mother told me this morning she would be frying chicken and making spaghetti, my favorite.

I knew I wasn't supposed to go up Greenside Street, but that was the only place I hadn't checked. As soon as I arrived at my destination, I saw who I was looking for. There was Manny right by the apartments. He was sitting on top of the mailbox by himself.

"Wassup dawg?!" I said to Manny, happy to see him.

"Big Ron, wassup with you, blood?"

"Um, just wondering where you been. We haven't seen you in school all week. No hard feelings from the other day, man. Just want you to know that," I said with sincerity.

"Preciate it cuz, but I'm not tripping off school at all. Good looking out, though," Manny said.

The thing about your childhood friends is that you could have an argument and bounce back from it like nothing happened. Girls tended to hold grudges, but not the fellas.

Manny had a preoccupied look on his face. His eyes wandered around a bit as if he was clocking everybody walking up and down the street. His eyes roamed the streets like an apex predator looking for prey.

"I'm going to the dinner dance next week with Evelyn," I said to Manny, crossing my arms to gage his reaction.

"What! You finally had the nuts to ask her, huh? You been liking that girl since the third grade!" Manny said.

"I just went for it, you know. In life, we have to go after what we want or regret it later," I said, sounding like a motivational speaker.

"Exactly! We have to go after what we want! That's what I been telling ya'll!" Manny said, but I had a feeling he was talking about something else entirely.

"Are you gonna go to the dinner dance?" I asked.

"Dinner dance?" Manny questioned.

"Yeah, dinner dance, man. Have you been listening to anything I been saying?" I asked in a frustrated tone.

"Oh yeah, but no, that's kids' stuff, bruh. Besides, I don't think I'm even going to graduate. And what I look like going to the dance if I'm not gonna walk the stage," Manny said.

"I feel you, but don't you think that you can talk to your teachers and see what work you're missing? I will help you catch up," I said.

"Look blood, I don't think this school thing is for me," Manny said.

"Manny, do you know what you are saying? If you drop out without an education, life will be ten times harder. You won't be able to get a good job because everybody will see you as a quitter."

Manny had a look on his face like he could care less. I wasn't going to be able to get through to him. I remember Manny for being the intelligent young boy he was. It wasn't that he wasn't smart; he just didn't feel that the school system would benefit him. Even I have questioned what the Oakland Unified School District was teaching us. They definitely didn't care about Black History—every year, the same people, Dr. Martin Luther King Jr., Harriet Tubman, Rosa Parks.

"Look man, just try the school thing out again. I don't want you to—"

Manny cut me off, saying, "The preacher preaches on Sunday!"

"What are you talking about?" I said.

"The preacher preaches on Sunday," he repeated.

"What does that even mean?" I asked.

"You are not a preacher, but yet you always trying to preach the gospel to me. You always trying to kick some game. Let the preacher preach on Sunday is all I'm saying. I never tell you how to do you!" Manny explained.

Manny had a slick tongue and a way of making something connect. I thought maybe he could be a great teacher, businessman, or even a stand-up comedian.

I took in everything that Manny just said and knew that there was no need to try to convince him. I knew that once Manny made up his mind about something it was already a done deal. I just wished he would put his determination and stubbornness toward something positive like getting a college degree or starting a business.

"Well, I ain't gonna try and convince you, bruh. But what you been up to?" I said.

"This," Manny said, with a devilish grin.

Manny already had his hand in his pocket and pulled out a neat stack of folded cash.

"Where did you get that from?" I asked.

"You asked where I been and what I been up to like you the po-lice or something. What you think?" Manny said to me like he was my elder.

"So you selling crack now, Manny? Really? You just gonna throw your life away?" I said.

"Not yet, bruh, I'm just a lookout. But I'm a couple hundred away from getting my own sack," Manny said.

"You are tripping, Manny!"

"You got it good, Ron, with both parents working hard to provide for you and your sister. My mom is just trying to find a baller to live off with her gold-digging ass. I'm tired of being the only one with food stamps when we go to the sto.' You said so yourself that we have to go after what we want!"

"Last week, we saw a dead body, Manny."

"Where?"

"Right there in front of King Estates. Some dude. They said he got shot during a drug deal."

"So!" Manny said.

"So? That's how you want to end up?"

"Here we go with the preaching again."

Manny pulled his cash all the way out of his pocket and ran his fingers through it. He ruffled through twenties, tens, and fives. I never seen anybody our age with that kind of cheese. Hell, my own daddy wasn't walking around with that kind of dough. In a short period of time, this little dude had accumulated more money than I had ever saved in my entire life.

My emotions were being pulled in different ways. I was torn between wanting to do the right thing, which was not sell dope, go to school, and live a good life, or post on the Ave. and start making that quick money. My folks gave me money, but not like that.

"I made enough money to buy *twenty* Super Soakers. Let me buy you one to make up for the other day," Manny said.

I wanted to slap that stupid smirk right off his face. "Nah, I'm cool. I'm Audi 5G. 'Bout to go home and eat. Guess I'll see you around," I said.

"Peace."

Manny threw up the peace sign as I sped up Greenside on my bike. As thoughts swirled in my head, I heard Manny yell toward the older D Boys, "There go the Po Po!"

Chapter 10

Curious for Cannabis

Is it gold, is it green, is it brown?
(No, it's Black C breaking them buds down)
Or should I say them indo clusters
Never want homegrown 'cause I'm an indo lover
Trip on the shit that I say
Or go take a trip to go get the shit
D to the A to the N to the K
(Niggas know what's up) So what more can I say?
If it's in a zag or a pipe
It's quite expensive, so you better smoke it right
Get a few niggas to fade
Find a cut, and just zurp in the shade
And like meat belongs to a meal
Grab a 40 with the dank 'cause it's time to get ill
It's better than crack cocaine
It ain't medicine, but it'll ease the pain
Don't give me no bammer weed
We don't smoke that shit in the SFC
Don't give me no bammer weed
We don't smoke that shit in the SFC

—"Don't Give Me No Bammer Weed," **RBL Posse**

We had been plotting on getting high for some time now. I mean everybody around the way was getting high. The war on drugs had made kids like me afraid of the repercussions. All through the neighborhoods were DARE signs. But not DARE, like I dare you to ring that doorbell and run, or my favorite kids' show, "Double Dare," but DARE stood for something. D.A.R.E. stood for Drug Abuse Resistance Education program.

My childhood was corrupted by Ronald Reagan. Reagan cut all the after-school programs in the hood. My father even lost his job because of Reagan.

Ronald Reagan and his wife Nancy Reagan led the war on drugs and they pushed a hard line. My father would say that Reagan was the worst thing that could ever happen to black folks and poor communities like ours. My father was right.

My father used to work for an organization called The Urban League. The Urban League helped people who didn't have resources and taught them how to look for jobs before the computer age. They also helped folks fill out applications, create resumes and cover letters, and practice interviewing. The Urban League was a God-send to poorer communities and Reagan cut the funding, subsequently, forcing my dad out of a job. The hate my father had for Ronald Reagan was too real.

During the Reagan administration, cops were locking up young black men and throwing away the key for petty drug violations. The Reagan administration imposed the war on drugs by targeting minorities and low-income communities. Reagan made the possession of five grams of crack carry a minimum five-year federal prison sentence compared to 500 grams of powder cocaine. That's 100 to 1. Why is this significant? Crack is being sold in the ghetto and powder cocaine is more prevalent in upscale neighborhoods with white folks. No one came out and said Ronald Reagan was a racist, but the writing was on the wall.

The Reagan administration had catchy phrases like "Just Say No" or "Crack Is Whack!" Jesse Jackson was famous for saying "Up with hope and down with dope!"

While I didn't have the urge to try dope, I was curious about weed. I just didn't know much about it.

Is weed just as bad as crack? Is weed a gateway drug? What does "gateway drug" even mean? Is a bag of weed at the gate, and when you walk up to the gate, the bag of weed grabs you and forces you to try other drugs like speed, PCP, heroin, and eventually crack?

I never heard of anyone overdosing on weed like basketball phenom Len Bias. I never heard of anyone doing sexual favors to score some weed. I never heard of people breaking into homes and selling the same stolen items around the neighborhood for a few measly dollars to score some weed.

In the minds of my friends and me, marijuana was a social thing. Hell, I could smell the weed aroma coming from the basement during my parents' house parties. In fact, I can't remember a house party that didn't have the sweet smell of ganja. It smelled good to me.

Evelyn would tell me that she hated walking in front of the liquor store on 76th and MacArthur because all of the D Boys down there were smoking bud and she hated the smell of it. She said the smell would get in her hair and clothes. I didn't mind the smell of a little weed. Little did I know that the weed smell was so pungent that I needed to be cautious or get caught?

I have always wanted to try it because it did not seem to have the effect crack did. It just made you mellow out. My curiosity got the best of my friends and me.

Scooter and I had a plan. We would pinch a little bit from our fathers' stashes until we had enough to roll a joint.

"Man, I don't know about this, Ron. What if my father finds out that I been going in his stash? He will whip my ass and you know it."

"Scoot, I don't think he is going to find out. From what you told me, he has a big ol' bag of it. Don't take too much and make it obvious, bruh," I said, trying to sound convincing.

"Why don't we just go down to the weed spot and cop a bag like everybody else. We could go to the Red Fence on 79th or Parker Street, or 77th Greenside, or 81st or 82nd and Dowling, or…" I had to cut Scooter off.

Yes, we lived in a community where weed was very easy to come by—the East Oakland epicenter for Mary Jane.

"Scooter, haven't you heard of cats getting robbed at the dope spot or killed at the dope spot? We're just kids. I ain't walking up on somebody's turf, saying, "Can I get a dime sack?"

"Why don't we ask Manny? I know you are not talking to him, but he has the line on everything else, from shoes to dope. I *know* he could get us some weed."

"Look man, I'm not asking Manny for no weed. I don't want him thinking that we are some desperate little kids trying to score a bag of weed. Like we need him or something. This is a one-time thing. We don't even know if we'll like it."

"All right, Ron. Just let me think about it. I'm already in hot water for that 'D' I got in Algebra. I've been working hard to bring up my grade. I don't need no more slip-ups."

Time went by, and before long, we had enough to roll a fat joint. Victor had stolen some Zig-Zags from his older brother. James said he wasn't down to smoke. We had to respect that. James wasn't the type to fold to peer pressure either.

It took us weeks of preparation, scheming, and plotting. I would have to wait until my dad left and go into the basement. That's where he kept his weed stash. I would take the smallest little weed bud that you could imagine, just a pinch. I pinched my father's weed stash ten times before I thought we had enough. My father had re-upped his stash several times in the course of me stealing from him. I was too nervous to steal the leftover doobies from his ashtray. He kept it all in an old Bally's shoe box, along with a pair of small scissors, a lighter, and a pack of Zig-Zags.

The master plan was foolproof. At least we thought it was. After school let out, we would wait until my parents left, go to my backyard shed, and fire it up. We would have enough time to air out and enjoy our high. Maybe go play "Sonic the Hedgehog" or "Mario Brothers."

I kept imagining getting caught by my dad. Maybe it would be like that one commercial with the white dad who finds his son's weed stash. The white dad burst into the room to confront his son and said, "Are these your drugs?"

"Look Dad, it's not mine—"

"Where did you get it? Answer me!"

"FROM YOU! ALL RIGHT, I LEARNED IT FROM WATCHING YOU!"

The white dad looked away from his son, with a devastated look on his face, filled with shame and guilt.

The black version would play out a little different.

"Are these your drugs?"

"Look Dad, it's not mine—"

"Where did you get it? Answer me!"

"FROM YOU! ALL RIGHT, I LEARNED IT FROM WATCHING YOU!"

In a rage, my father would first slap me. Then he would beat the shit out of me and proceed to choke me until I had no more air in my body. My mother would come into my bedroom and try to pry my dad's hands off my lifeless little frame.

I thought I liked the white version better.

I thought we could pull this off, though. The key would be not getting caught. Most of the time, I stayed out of trouble to avoid a whipping from my dad. That alone kept me from doing wrong...most of the time.

Maybe this was a bad idea. Maybe I should have been more like James and not have any interest in weed or alcohol. After all, I was an athlete, and if I wanted to play high school basketball, I would have to take care of my body. I shouldn't be messing my body up with drugs and stuff, but what's one time going to hurt?

I always heard adults tell me to enjoy my childhood. They say you only get a chance to be a kid once. Don't grow up too fast. Is this what they meant? Am I trying to do the things I see adults doing? I clearly wasn't ready for sex, but weed is different. I bet the Native Americans smoked a little in the peace pipe every now and then. I weighed the pros and cons, but eventually my curiosity won out.

We were on the bus making our way home from school. I was excited, yet nervous, at the same time. Scooter was, too. I could tell. Victor seemed to be ready. James had stopped trying to talk us out of it. He knew it was a lost cause.

"Are you sure your folks will be gone long enough, Ron?" Scooter asked.

"Yeah, bro, it will be fine. We just act like we're playing until they bounce and then it's on."

We hung out in front of Scooter's house until time came for my parents to take my sister Leah to her doctor's appointment. I went to check in with my parents.

"Did you finish your homework?" my mother asked.

"Yes Mom. I finished my homework during lunch. I didn't have that much."

"That's my boy," my dad said.

"There's plenty of that leftover spaghetti from last night. If you get hungry, just heat some up."

"I think I will. Bye ya'll. See you later."

I kissed my sister on the forehead, and they jumped in the car and pulled off. I felt confident that they didn't suspect anything. I could be a good actor when I wanted to be. I'm sure that's how adults who are good liars get started. We kids practice getting over on our parents, and we get so good at it that it carries over into adulthood.

I motioned to the fellas to come over to my house. Victor and Scooter ran over to my house. James came over reluctantly.

"Big James!" we all cheered.

"You in on this? You want to see what it's all about, huh?" Victor said.

"Nah, I'm just going to be the lookout. I can't let ya'll get into trouble before O.N.B.L." O.N.B.L. stood for the Oakland Neighborhood Basketball League. We were defending champions.

"Aww James, just one time," Scooter said.

"Nah, I'm cool," James replied.

There was no point in trying to convince James, and I was happy that he would help us.

We went to my backyard by the shed. The shed had a small section behind it, where a small group of people could fit. The wooden fence at the very back visually protected us from the outside world.

Scooter reached into his pocket. "This is what I have," he said.

"That's perfect. I have about the same. It's enough to roll into a joint. Victor, did you remember to grab the Zig-Zags?"

"You know it. Here they are. Ya'll want me to roll? I watched my older brother do it a couple of times," Victor said.

"Cool, because I don't know how to roll," I said.

"All right, break it down," Victor said, sounding like someone well beyond his years.

Scooter and I broke the bud down and handed it to Victor. We watched as he put the weed in the Zig-Zag. He gently maneuvered the weed into an even amount spread throughout the paper. He pushed some around with his finger until it was even and ready to be twisted. He was good. It looked as if he had been rolling weed his whole life.

"You sure this is your first time?" Scooter asked.

"You're too good at this."

"Just observation, man," Victor said.

He twisted the paper together, licked the sticky part, and folded it over with his index fingers and thumbs.

"All set," Victor said.

"Fire it up!" I said excitedly.

"Fire it up!" Victor said, passing me the unlit joint.

"I don't have a lighter. I thought you would bring one, Vic," I said.

"I just said I was bringing the Zags, bruh. Don't put that on me. Scoot, do you have a lighter or matches or anything?"

"Nope. I ain't got nothing. Ron, run in the house and grab your dad's lighter real quick."

"All right, wait here."

I ran into the house to grab the lighter. I couldn't believe that after all this planning and we had forgotten to grab something to light the joint with. What amateurs. What rookies we were.

I started to panic because I did not see my dad's lighter in the usual place in the basement. Think Ron, think. I knew my mother kept matches for her candles somewhere, maybe in the kitchen drawer. I looked through the kitchen drawer and eventually found a book of matches. I must have been gone for about 10 minutes. Then I ran to the backyard shed.

"Took you long enough... My dad is going to be home in a little while. Give me that lighter," Scooter said. He already had the joint in his hand as if he was Snoop Dogg or somebody.

"I couldn't find a lighter. I found matches."

"Same thing—fire it up," Victor said.

We had much practice with matches lighting firecrackers as kids. Scooter struck a match and put it to the end of the joint. The powerful weed aroma filled the tiny elevated area we stood in. Scooter took a deep inhale and blew out a thick cloud of smoke. He coughed, and coughed, hard. I was kind of nervous to hit it after that. What did he expect his first time?

"Hit it lightly," Scooter said and passed it to Victor.

Victor hit the joint and the same thing happened. He passed me the joint and I tried to hit it lightly, but I coughed as if I had something stuck in my throat. I thought I was going to die. The neighbors had to be hearing what was going on.

Surprisingly, after about three or four rounds, we all were hitting the weed without coughing. I felt my high kicking in. All of my senses were heightened. Touch, smell, hearing, and vision. I hadn't had a chance to test my taste, but I heard it made food taste better.

We smoked and laughed. Our eyes were watery from coughing so much. Paranoia had begun to kick in from the pot.

"You hear that?" I asked.

"I don't hear nothing," Victor said.

"James is out there. He'll yell or something. You fools are just paranoid."

We passed the joint around a couple more times, and all of a sudden, I heard James's voice booming from the side of the house. Or maybe I was tripping again.

"I know ya'll heard that?" I whispered.

"Yeah, that's James talking to somebody. I know his voice. Maybe just talking to the neighbor," Scooter said.

Then we all heard clear as day. "I think our baseball landed back there, Mr. Anderson." James was practically shouting to alert us.

"Oh shit. What are we gonna do?" Victor asked.

I snatched the joint out of his hands and threw it over the fence. We dusted off our shirts. I was going to come out and put on an act. I thought Scooter and Victor were right behind me. And then I looked back and saw both of them going over the fence. They were gone in seconds. I stepped from behind the shed to lock eyes with my father.

"Hey umm…that was a quick doctor's appointment." I must have looked like I had seen a ghost.

"Damn secretary gave us the wrong date. Drove to North Oakland for nothing. Did you find the ball?"

"The ball…oh yeah, I think it might be on the other side of this fence in our neighbor's backyard. I believe Scooter and Vic are over there looking for it now."

"Oh…okay," my father said, with a questioning look on his face. Then he sniffed and his eyes looked from side to side as if he was trying to figure out the aroma.

"It smells like reefer back here."

"Reefer?" I said.

"Yeah, reefer. You heard me."

"What the heck is reefer?" I asked my dad, knowing damn well I knew what reefer was. I used to hear the OGs say it on MacArthur. They would say it like "Pass the reefer, Young Blood." They were so cool with it. Meanwhile, my father looked like a strict private investigator getting ready to interrogate me.

"You know...weed, marijuana, reefer... I smell it back here," he said, looking directly at me to see if I was going to lie to him. Luckily, my eyes weren't red yet.

"Dad, I have no idea where the smell is coming from. It's probably coming from next door. You know how they get down. Let me tell James I can't find the ball," I said, starting to motion to the backyard gate, where James was waiting.

Did my father buy it? It felt like time was going by super slow as I awaited my father's response. Was it really taking him this long to answer? Was it the weed? Is he going to kill me?

He finally said, "Yeah, you're right. They keep a party going over there, and I know my son ain't fool enough to smoke weed in my backyard. You got two more hours to hang out—then get your butt back in the house. You got school tomorrow."

"All right, Dad. I won't be out too long. I know it's a school night."

I must have run past him so fast he couldn't get a whiff of my shirt. James was waiting for me outside. We hurried away from the backyard.

"Did he bust you?" James asked.

"Nah, I played it off smooth."

"Well...how do you feel?"

"I feel like everything is moving in slow motion. In the backyard, we were laughing at stuff that wasn't even funny," I said.

"I don't feel in control at all. In fact, as we walk down this street, it feels like everybody is staring at us. Do you think they know I'm high?" I asked, with wide eyes.

"How could they know? Your dad didn't figure it out, so you're good. I just always thought of you as one of the smart ones, Ron."

"I just wanted to try it. It's not crack," I said, starting to get annoyed.

"Yeah, but it's been known to lead to other drugs, harder drugs."

"You're right, James," I said just to get him to shut up.

Just then the ice cream truck came down our street. I heard it before I saw it. Some other kids ran up to it. I would kill for a Neapolitan ice cream sandwich or push-up, but I was broke.

Victor and Scooter were hanging out in front of Victor's house. I could smell rice, beans, and spices coming from Victor's home. Their eyes were red by this point.

"Hey ya'll eyes are red. Do mine's look like that?"

"Kind of. You must didn't hit it hard enough."

"You saw me hit it hard. Maybe I'm not a professional like you two, Mister Cheech and Mister Chong," I said.

We laughed for about 5 minutes straight at my subpar joke. We were hunched over in laugher, as James just stared at us.

"That wasn't even that funny," James said.

"Shut up, party pooper," Scooter said.

Again, we started laughing and slapping our knees like Eddie Murphy had just delivered a punch line. My high had fully kicked in by now. I felt relaxed and giddy. Things still seemed to be moving slowly around me.

"I'll be right back. I think my brother has some Visine," Victor said.

"You are a lifesaver," Scooter said.

Victor returned with the Visine and we took turns dripping it into our eyes. Since none of us wore glasses and never had to deal with contacts, it was hard putting it in our eyes. By the time we finished, half the Visine bottle was gone and our faces looked like we had been crying. We had Visine-soaked faces.

"Visine is supposed to go in your eyes and not your face," James said.

We laughed uncontrollably at his mediocre joke. It was too funny, and I started to get the sense that James was getting irritated with our antics.

"Ya'll are trippin'. I'm out of here," James said as he left.

We all mocked James. "James, don't go. Please don't go, James. Ha ha ha."

James had about as much as he could take. He did help us even though he didn't participate. James was not a follower and we had much gratitude for his leadership now and later in life.

"Victor, your house is smelling hella good right now," I said.

"It sure is," Scooter said.

"My parents really like you guys and think we're good kids. Let me see if I could grab ya'll some grub," Victor said and went inside the house.

When Victor returned, he was carrying two plates. One was stacked with quesadillas and the other plate was nachos stacked with carne asada, cheese, sour cream, guacamole, and jalapenos.

"Vic, you came through!" I said.

"Gracias, mi hermano," Scooter said.

"De nada."

For the next 20 minutes, we ate and laughed. We had the munchies bad, which made the food taste twice as good. We cleaned both plates and licked our fingers. My friends were *mi familia.* Nothing could separate us unless you were like Manny and decided that money was more important than your boys.

The sun began to make its way down. The sun rises in the east, but sets in the west. It was a beautiful end to a day.

Ultimately, I decided marijuana was not for me. I didn't like all the hiding and how you smelled afterwards. I didn't like the fact that everything seemed funny when it really wasn't. I was going to be applying for jobs in a couple of years, and what if they drug-tested me? This was a stupid idea. I needed to be in control of my life and my destiny. Smoking marijuana did not make me feel like I'm in control. I guess it's like James said.

Chapter 11

White Vernacular

Childhood remembrances are always a drag if you're Black
You always remember things like living in Woodlawn
With no inside toilet and if you become famous or something
They never talk about how happy you were to have your
Mother all to yourself and
How good the water felt when you got your bath
From one of those
Big tubs that folk in Oakland barbecue in
And somehow when you talk about home
It never gets across how much you
Understood their feelings
As the whole family attended meetings about Hollydale
And even though you remember
Your biographers never understand
Your father's pain as he sells his stock
And another dream goes
And though you're poor it isn't poverty that
Concerns you
And though they fought a lot it isn't your father's drinking that
Makes any difference
But only that everybody is together and you
And your sister have happy birthdays and very good
Christmases
And I really hope no white person ever has cause
To write about me

Because they never understand
Black love is Black wealth and they'll probably talk about my
Hard childhood and never understand that all the while I was
Quite happy

—"Nikki-Rosa," *Black Feeling, Black Talk, Black Judgment,*
Nikki Giovanni

My mom inspired me in many ways to be the best I could be. I was trying to find my place in this world as a young African American boy. This was a tall task because my friends were always riding me for not being hood enough. They knew I had heart. They knew I wasn't afraid to fight, but I and James actually tried to do well in school. They made fun of the fact that I used to talk like a white boy. Now I've been running the streets for so long that I no longer sounded like a white boy, but they still remembered there was a time. Your friends don't let you forget.

Three years ago, Scooter, Manny, Victor, James, and I went to Earl's tenth birthday party. The party was decked out and Earl's mom pulled out all the stops. Earl's uncle was barbequing in the backyard. You could smell the ribs and chicken all the way down the street. Earl only lived half a block down. We had all gone to school with Earl since the first grade. Earl didn't always hang with us, but we still thought he was one of us.

We heard there was going to be a piñata and plenty of food, so we made sure to be at Earl's party. When we arrived at Earl's house, we were greeted by Earl's auntie. "Can I help you?" Earl's aunt asked.

"Yes ma'am. Is Earl home? We were invited to his party?" I said reluctantly, since nobody else wanted to speak up.

"Yes, he is. What a nice group of young men. Please come in," Earl's auntie said.

I had never been inside Earl's house before and didn't really have any expectations for the place. Plastic covered the couches in the living room. I thought that people were not allowed to sit on these couches because the living room looked like a museum.

"Come back to my bedroom," Earl said.

As we walked past his younger cousins, uncles, and aunts, we walked through the kitchen on our way to Earl's bedroom in the back. On the kitchen table was one of the biggest cakes I had ever seen. It looked like a wedding cake. I blurted out, "THIS CAKE IS HUMONGOUS!"

I heard the adults in the kitchen giggle after I said it.

"What does humongous mean?" Earl asked.

"It's like big or large," I said.

"Well, why didn't you just say big or large?" Scooter asked.

"It's so plain to use common words. I try to use a new word every day," I proclaimed, remembering what my mother had told me about how important it was to have a strong vocabulary.

"Ron's mama is a librarian, so he is always using fancy words," Victor said.

"Dude, I'm not always using fancy words," I said, getting irritated.

"Dude, I'm not always using fancy words," Manny then said, mocking me.

The homies all laughed at me. When I went away to summer camps, I was not around other black boys like me in the hood and it rubbed off on me. I was starting to talk like my rich summer camp friends. I couldn't help it.

"Ya'll chill out. You see Ron getting mad. Why don't ya'll stall him out, blood?" James said. "Stall him out" was code for giving someone a break.

Of course James had my back. We were both undercover nerds at heart.

We hung out in Earl's room playing Nintendo. We each took a turn until we got bored. Earl suggested that we go play in the backyard while there was still daylight. Earl had a brand-new football he had gotten from his uncle, so we played catch with it, seeing who could throw the best spiral.

We played catch until Scooter suggested we play three flies up. Earl's backyard was just big enough to play. In three flies up, the first person to catch the ball three times wins. All of my friends were competitive, but Scooter stood out.

"I'll be the quarterback," Earl said.

The rest of us huddled by the back fence fighting for position while Earl threw Hail Mary's one at a time until James exuberantly yelled out that he had three catches. We all won a round, except Victor. Victor was probably the least athletic out of all of us. He was also the shortest. I felt bad for him at times.

"Food is ready. You boys go wash your hands in the bathroom," Earl's uncle said.

There was no way they were going to let us start chowing down without washing up, especially after we had been playing in the grass and dirt.

We stormed through the house and formed a single-file line at the bathroom downstairs, taking turns washing our hands. We made plates in the kitchen, but were told to eat outside with the rest of the kids.

I had a few ribs, some chicken, and potato salad and baked beans. I had no vegetables on my plate. Hell, my mom is not here to tell me otherwise.

The food was amazing and I had overeaten. I had that overly stuffed feeling, but I wasn't the only one. Everybody at the party was moving slow.

We sat and talked about school, sports, and video games. That was the only thing on a ten year old's mind in those days. I noticed one of the aunties playing close attention to everything we were saying. I wondered why she was being so nosey. We weren't cussing or saying anything out of the ordinary. We all knew how to "fake it" in front of adults. If we cursed, it was when we were out in the streets.

We made sure to talk politely in front of adults. We especially put on a front in front of teachers, acting one way in the hood and acting another way at school. Later, I would learn that this was called "code switching" and people did it at work, too.

The sun was starting to go down and it was getting close to the time to go. I had drunk too much orange Tang. I used the bathroom one last time. When I came out of the bathroom, I overheard a lady, who was eavesdropping on our conversation all night, say, "Yeah, I think the little one with the light blue shirt on thinks he is better than everybody. He thinks he knows everything, too."

Wait…What? I was the only one with a light blue shirt on. Why was she talking about me when I was just a kid? I hadn't done anything to anybody. She didn't even know me. I decided to be quiet and listen in the hallway where nobody could see me.

"Awe, Renee, don't be so hard on the boys. They are only thirteen years old. Besides what's wrong with talking proper?" asked Earl's aunt.

"I just don't like it. If I closed my eyes and just listened to him talk, I would swear up and down it was a white boy talking," she said.

"There's nothing wrong with that. Talking ghetto ain't going to get you a good job and you know that. That's the problem with black folks today. People think you have to use street slang to show how real you are," Earl's auntie said. Earl's auntie had known me since I was born.

Just then I started feeling a tingling in my eyes as they began to water. I didn't want anybody to see me crying, so I ran back into the bathroom before somebody else had to use it. I dried my eyes and tried to convince myself that she hadn't hurt my feelings.

I knew I sounded different than my friends, but I didn't know it was that obvious. I blamed my mom and dad for always taking me to Berkeley and the Oakland Hills for swimming lessons, summer camp, and college preparatory programs. I blamed my father for always correcting me when I said ain't, hella, wanna, finna, boutstoo, and all the other broken English that was native to our hood.

I slipped down the hallway and back to the outside without the adults even noticing me. The fellas were getting ready to leave.

"I thought you bounced already, Ron," Manny said.

"No man, just talking to one of Earl's family members," I lied.

"You were probably in the bathroom blowing it up. All that BBQ, huh?" Scooter joked, and the gang giggled.

"You know me. I'm going to head out ya'll. Thanks again for the invite, Earl," I said, as I walked on the side of the house to avoid seeing any of the adults.

I didn't want to sound like a white boy. I wanted my speech to be in tune with who I truly was. I knew who I was, but if other people saw me as proper, then I needed to change or be a target in the hood.

As I walked home, I thought about all the times my mother and father had corrected me when I used slang. They told me that I couldn't get a good job if I spoke hood slang. They told me that in order to make it in this world that I had to speak the "King's English."

My friends didn't tease me about it that much because they knew how angry it made me. What if I was cornered by some of the older D Boys and they made me a target because I wasn't black enough? I was always rocking Black and Proud T-shirts, dashikis, Malcolm X T-shirts, and African medallions, and yet some people were still questioning my blackness? I couldn't believe it.

I was black enough, but maybe not how they saw blackness. If they wanted ghetto black, then I would give them ghetto black. From this point on, I was thinking, NOBODY will ever question my blackness because of how I talk. I will have the slickest tongue. If they want slang, then I will give them slang! If they want Ebonics, then I will give them Ebonics. I ain't no damn white boy. I'm a black boy from the hood.

I had this conversation with myself when I was ten years old. I was thirteen now. I cursed more in regular conversation. I used poor English because I was shown that this is what it takes to be black. Is it who I am deep down on the inside? Probably not, but I have to do what I have to do to survive. Ain't nobody going to make fun of me for sounding like a white boy ever again.

That was until my mom convinced me to enter a writing contest at the Festival at the Lake.

Chapter 12

Festival at the Lake

Really doe, a sunny day, I'm playing for keeps

No need for a rental, a bicycles cool, because my
game is deep

A freak peeped, and looked sweet by the lakeside

She was going to her friends to go on a bike ride

So we went, we rode, she bent my pole

Met her a minute ago now this heffer I can't control

Is it because my billboard flicks, tone got the real long
crisps

Three times crazy (man I know this)

Ager I feel ya, but some others don't

I'm bippin' fools off the weed smoke, selling they gats
for C-notes

And then I hit the strip and parked the bike by the
curb

Regal was coming to snatch me, Man, I was kind of
happy, word

This 24 is like one of a kind

In the O-A-K where I chill and parlay in the sunshine

—"Sunshine in the O," **3X KRAZY**

Lake Merritt is a beautiful manmade lake in the heart of downtown Oakland. It is about three miles all the way around. I went to a boating camp when I was eight years old at Lake Merritt. The lake was filled with ducks, geese, pelicans, and all kinds of beautiful birds.

My mother would take me bike riding around Lake Merritt and she loved it just as much as I did. On one occasion, we were bike riding and I thought I was hot stuff and told my mom I would take a different path than her. I yelled to my mom that I would meet her at the car. Well, I got lost that night and learned a valuable lesson that if you are unsure of which direction you are going then you should probably stay with someone familiar with the area.

I decided to write a short story about my experience, but instead of me being the main character, I would use my little sister. I wasn't ready to admit to the world that I had gotten lost at Lake Merritt.

My short story was called "Lost at the Lake" and my parents really dug it. They convinced me to enter my story into the Festival at the Lake young writers' competition, and I won second place. I was juiced, because as second place, I could choose from a $100 gift certificate at Sears or a $50 gift certificate at Sizzler. Who would want steak when I might be able to buy video games or a remote-control car?

Every year they would have the Festival at the Lake and the lake would be poppin' with hella black folks wearing their best clothes. All of the boys were trying to talk to the girls and hopefully get a phone number. The girls were just trying to be seen. It wasn't that the girls were trying to meet a nice guy, but they got dressed up, so they could outshine all the other girls.

I thought it was funny how folks would dress up to impress other people and not just for the sake of looking good for your own self-confidence. Little did I know I would be doing the same thing in high school?

I made the gang swear that they wouldn't tell anybody in the neighborhood that I had won second place in a writing contest. If the D Boys knew I could write and actually cared about school, they would kick my ass up and down 78th Avenue, so I decided to keep this within the crew. I made them take a blood oath. But that still didn't stop them from teasing me before the festival.

We caught the 57 bus to the lake and it was filled with vendors selling arts and crafts. People were selling clothes that looked handmade. I wasn't really into tie-dye shirts, but I knew how to make them, because I learned it at Arts Camp. The other vendors were selling paintings, drawings, pottery, music albums, African drums, and tons of other things.

I loved the Festival at the Lake because it brought everybody out. Oakland is mostly black, but during the festival, everybody and their mama was out enjoying the beautiful weather and people. It wasn't just a black thing, but rather an *everybody* thing.

"Bruh, did you see that girl in the all-black biker shorts?" I asked the boys.

"Yeah man, she was hella fine!" Scooter said.

"Why didn't you holler at her? I bet she would have given you the number," James said.

"I thought we were going to walk around a bit and see who's here?" I said.

"You just sprung off Evelyn so stop lying. That's why you didn't say nothing," Victor said, busting me out.

"Shut up, Victor. I have never seen you talk to a girl, except to ask to borrow a pencil at school." I got a laugh from the rest of the fellas.

"Victor, you are rather timid around girls. You need to come out your shell. You scared?" James said.

"Hell nah, blood! I ain't scared of girls!"

"You sure? Show us!" Scooter said.

We laughed as Victor approached girl after girl, getting shot down each time. I was able to deflect from my infatuation with Evelyn and get my friends to focus on Victor's lack of game.

"Victor, you can't just come out and ask for the girl's number," James said.

"I told you I wasn't scared though!" Victor replied.

"Okay, okay, you're not scared, but now I'm worried that you don't have any game. And we can't have you hanging with us if you don't know how to talk to girls. Now watch the master at work," Scooter said, as he approached a tall light-skinned girl with big hoop earrings. She had on blue Guess overall shorts and white K-Swiss sneakers.

"I love how your earrings match your bracelet. I'm Jermaine. These are my friends," he said. We all gave a half wave to her and her friends. Scooter was too smooth. He had no problem talking with girls.

James, Victor, and I walked over and started talking to her friends. I was talking to one of her friends who told me her name was Danielle. She was cute, but could not hold a candle to Evelyn. I could tell she wanted me to ask for the number, so I did. She didn't hesitate to give it to me.

"See, that's how you do it, Victor," Scooter bragged.

"You too cocky, blood," Victor said, unimpressed.

"I'm not cocky. I'm just trying to give you some game, blood."

"It's all good. Your opening line was dope, though," Victor said.

"See that's the key. Compliment their hair or outfit, or comment on something silly you both can see or have noticed. Once you get them to smile and talk back to you, you're in. Some girls like playing hard to get, but I've even seen some of them soften up."

"Did I hear you use your government name, *Jermaine*?" I teased.

"Oh you got jokes?" Scooter said.

"Hi, I'm *Jermaine*," James mocked.

"Ain't no girl going to respect you if you roll up talking about your name is Scooter. I'll tell her my nickname once I get to know her a little better. That's if I call her. Ha ha ha," Scooter said. He was really feeling himself now.

154

We walked through the food court area and they had all kinds of food vendors: Mexican, Greek, Chinese, Burgers, and BBQ. We all got bacon-wrapped hot dogs and soda. It might have been the best hot dog I ever had in my life.

Just then, I looked up in time to see the Dope Boys from our block: Tremaine, Baron, Blac. I guess they took time off from grinding on Mac to have some fun.

"Well, if it ain't nappy-head Ron and the squares. That should be the name of your singing group, Nappy-Head Ron and the Three Squares. Ha ha ha," Baron said, laughing at his own joke.

"Wassup ya'll," I said back. They weren't going to mess up this day for me.

"Where's Raymond?" James said.

"He's on a little vacation right now," Tremaine said.

This was code for being locked up. He's probably in Juvenile Hall. Getting locked up was nothing to these guys. They were in and out of jail all the time. Jail had zero effect on them. They had a dismal outlook on life.

"It's poppin' at this year's festival. Did ya'll meet any chicken heads?" Blac asked.

"As a matter of fact, we did," Scooter said, as he pulled out a fist full of phone numbers scribbled on torn-up pieces of paper.

"Oh snap. You scrubs think ya'll got game. I ain't even mad at ya'll," Blac said.

It was refreshing to get props from the older homies. We had always tried to avoid them.

"Where you guys going now?" Baron said.

"Ron has to go…"

"I have to go to the bathroom." I cut Victor off from spilling the beans about my writing competition. Things were going good today and I wanted it to stay that way.

"See ya'll back in the 700 zone," Tremaine said.

I loved seeing all the different kinds of people. Oakland is so diverse and this was a showcase of so many different kinds of people getting together. I love the Festival at the Lake!

"It's almost 3:00, Ron. Don't you have to go to the west stage for your prize?" James asked.

"Oh crap. Let's head over," I said.

My homeboys and I made it over to the west stage. There was a table of older-looking white people sitting behind a table by the stage. I thought they must be who I had to talk to.

I walked over to them and introduced myself. "Hi, I'm Ronald Anderson," I said in my best school voice.

"You are an excellent writer, young man," an older man said to me.

"Thank you, sir."

"Have you thought about going to college and taking creative writing?" he asked.

"I have thought about college, but I haven't figured out what I want to major in yet. I still have time."

"Yes, you do, but that time will be here before you know it," a lady at the table chimed in.

Then she said, "Hi, I'm Patrice. I am a librarian from the Oakland Main Library and I was one of the judges."

"Nice to meet you, Ms. Patrice," I said.

"Would you like to read your story this afternoon?"

I was hoping they wouldn't ask me to read my story. But I would just be reading it and it's not like I had to memorize and recite it. So why was I nervous? I read in front of my homeboys all the time at school.

"Sure," I finally said.

They handed me a copy of my story, and I walked back to where my boys were standing.

"So wassup? Did they cut you a check yet?" Scooter asked, repeating something he heard on TV.

"Gift certificate, bruh. No, they haven't given it to me yet."

"What were they up there asking you about, blood?" Victor asked.

"Nothing really. Asking what I want to study when I go to college."

"I'm not going to college. My folks are going to be happy enough with me graduating from high school," Victor said.

"Victor, you are really smart and I seen you taking stuff apart and putting it back together. Stuff I could *never* do. You could be an engineer. Do you have any idea how much money engineers make?" I asked.

"Engineers clock grip, Vic!" James said.

"Really?" Victor said.

"Yeah, really, and you are not going to become an engineer with just a high school diploma. You could work at the taco truck on East 14th," I said.

"Do you really think I could go to college?" Victor asked.

"Absolutely—we are *all* smart in different ways, Vic. You have to realize your potential, man," I said.

"Will you show me how to apply and all that?"

"Of course. *Tu eres mi hermano!*" I said.

"What you say, Ron?" Scooter asked.

"I said he's my brother. All of ya'll are my brothers!" I said proudly.

The first-place winner had finished reading her short story and it was my turn. I was no longer nervous and my friends had my back. When I looked up, I saw Leah sitting on my mom's lap. I didn't even know they had come. I was elated to read my story in front of my family and best friends. I wrote this story and I was proud. I'm not hiding my talent from anybody. I like books. I like to write and I don't care who knows.

After I finished reading my short story, the crowd gave me a nice round of applause. It gave me goose pimples, but I thought, this might be something I could get used to. I walked over to my mom to give her and my little sister a hug.

"You did good, Ronny," my mom said.

"Thanks, Mom. I learned from you."

"You boys ready to go?"

"Yes Ms. Anderson," my friends said in unison.

The Festival at the Lake was over, but a ton of people didn't want the party to end. People were just hanging out and the boys were starting to be aggressive toward the girls.

We followed my mom to the car and piled in. As we drove down Grand Lake Avenue, we all looked out of the window to see a group of girls running from some guys who were chasing them. The guys stopped chasing them when they saw the girls running toward the cops on the corner.

My mother was trying to get to the freeway so we could head back to East Oakland. The only problem was there was traffic at the intersection of Grand Lake and Harrison Street.

"I wonder what's going on up there," James said.

"I'll bet you anything there is a sideshow going down," I said.

We all sat up straight so we could see down the street. Just then a gold Pontiac Firebird illegally drove on the side of us, slappin' MC Breed's "Ain't No Future in Your Frontin'." His 15-inch speakers shook my mom's rear-view mirror and her whole car. There wasn't any lane on the side of us, but the Pontiac made room.

When the Pontiac got to the intersection, he didn't wait for permission. He didn't ask for his turn. He put the pedal to the metal and let loose. The homies and I were looking in amazement. All four tires on the Pontiac were smoking like a chimney.

"See, I told you it was going to go down! We should have stayed a little a longer."

"Man, this is icing on the cake," Scooter said.

We watched the Pontiac spin perfect doughnuts until the police came. It took another 10 minutes for the intersection to completely clear out. My mom just shook her head with disapproval.

Some people say that The Town is dangerous. Some people say The Town is violent. Some people say The Town is diverse. Some People say The Town beautiful. I say, it ain't NOTHING like The Town!

Chapter 13

I Ain't Ready!

What we have here is subject to controversy

A three-letter word some regard as a curse, see

He may fiend and have a wet dream

Because he seen a teen in tight jeans

What makes him react like that is biological

But scheme of gettin' in those jeans, is diabolical

But of course he does it, and she gives him rap

And before you even know it, they jump in the sack

As a matter of fact, sometimes it's like that

But anyway, ready or not, here he cums

And like a dumb son-of-a-gun, oops, he forgot the condoms

"Oh well," you say, "what the hell, it's chill

I won't get got, I'm on the pill"

Until the sores start to puff and spore

He gave it to you, and now it's yours

Let's talk about sex, baby (sing it)
Let's talk about you and me (sing it, sing it)
Let's talk about all the good things
And the bad things that may be

—"Let's Talk About Sex," **Salt-N-Pepa**

She said her mom was working late and we would have the house to ourselves. I was nervous and didn't want to mess up my first time. All I knew about sex was that we needed a condom or Evelyn would be pregnant.

I flashed back to an earlier time when I went over to my mom's friend, Maxine's, house two summers ago. Maxine had a daughter we called Char, short for Charlene.

My mom and Maxine were known to talk for hours at a time. When we went over to Maxine's house, I had comic books to read and my game boy. Maxine's daughter, Char, was always excited to see me. She was a tomboy and we had some classic basketball games around the corner from her house in North Oakland.

Char was twelve years old, and already had the body of a grown woman. With Char's height and size, she was a challenge on the basketball court. I could still beat her because of my solid jumper, speed, and handles.

"What's going on, scrub?" Char said.

"Scrub? Last time I checked, I whipped you in twenty-one last summer," I recanted back.

"Twenty-one to seventeen—I hardly call that a whipping," Char said to me.

"Well, if I had my basketball shoes, I would serve you again. Give you that Tim Hardaway Killer Crossover!"

"More like Killer Rollover. You wish you were Tim Hardaway! I am still 2 inches taller than you last time I checked."

I hated the fact that girls had their growing spurt before boys. I hated the fact that girls hit puberty before boys. I hated the fact that girls knew more than boys. It felt like they had a head start. It wasn't fair.

Char had developed into a full-fledged woman with an hourglass shape. She was five-nine and thick. Her breasts were full and pronounced. She wore tight jeans to accentuate the curves in her hips and booty. Her hair was braided like Janet Jackson's. She was fine, but was more like a sister to me since we knew each other since I was four years old.

I was five-four and weighed in at 105 pounds. My Uncle Charles said I had a bird chest on the account that I was so skinny. My growing spurt had not happened yet, and it was painfully obvious. My skinny frame sometimes affected my confidence.

Char was looking at me in a different way today. Could it be my crisp fade I was sporting? Could it be my button-up, light blue church shirt and slacks? I didn't know what she was thinking, but it didn't look like sports.

"You ever played house?" Char inquired.

"No, but I heard about it. You played before?" I responded as I tried to play off the fact that I had no idea how to play house.

"I played with my friend before. It's just make- believe. You pretend to be grown, that's all."

"Pretend to be grown?" I asked reluctantly.

"Yeah. I'll be the mom and you be the dad. Like make-believe," Char explained.

"Um, I don't know, Char. Maybe we can play basketball, after all. I can play in my church shoes. You really have no excuse if I school you in my church clothes," I said.

"I don't want to play basketball, Ron. Play house with me," Char said, with a slight pout.

"Umm…sure," I said, but not really knowing what I was getting into.

"Let's use these two couches over here as our home. We could throw a blanket over the top and make a hut. It will be our home. I just need to get the blankets from my room." She left to retrieve the blankets from her room.

When Char came back into the living room, she had three huge blankets folded up in her arms. "Help me move these two couches closer together so we can throw the blanket over," she said.

"Um… All right," I replied.

We pushed the couches closer to each other. Char draped the blanket over the top of the two facing couches. It looked like we were going camping. She then laid a blanket on the bottom of our indoor hut.

Charlene had prepped our fake home to make it look comfortable. She added some pillows to the floor and called it our pretend bedroom. What would my mom and Ms. Maxine think? We were just kids being kids, right?

"Rest your head on the pillow, Ron. You have had a long day at work," Char said.

"Uh huh?"

"Make-believe, Ron. Remember?" Char said.

My heart began to race. I didn't know where this was going. I didn't know how to make-believe being somebody's husband. What was Charlene really up to?

"Uh, okay," I said.

I was a nervous wreck. But I didn't want to show Char that I was. I tried to play it cool and rolled over like a dog on the pillow and barked.

"You are so silly. That's what I always liked about you," Char said in a flirty manner.

"Fa real, Charlene?" I said.

"Yeah. Now lie down and play sleep. I'll do the same."

With my heart skipping a beat, I lay down and put my head on the pillow. What was going to happen next? How long was I supposed to lay here? What was the point of this house game? Maybe I should have asked these questions before committing to playing the game.

Charlene pulled up close to me. I could feel her ample breast on my back. My pants began to form a tent from my stiff erection. I remembered this feeling from when I saw the white lady's boobs in the movie, *Police Academy.* My joint was swollen and I was embarrassed. I didn't want Char to see my hard wood.

Char moved in closer and slid her hand inside my Fruit of the Loom underwear and grabbed my hard dick in her hands. I had a rush of sensations, from excitement to panic to fear. Still, it felt so good. Was this the beginning of having sex? I always heard about it, but at that point was still clueless.

She held her hands there for several seconds and then abruptly turned on her back side. "Now you put your hands in mine," Char instructed.

"But Charlene I never…"

"It's okay. I'll show you."

"What if…"

"Make-believe, remember," she said, as if that would relieve my anxiety.

My palms were beginning to clam up and I didn't want Char to feel my sweaty hands. I quickly wiped them off on my pants the best I could. I was going to do it. I was scared, but I was no punk.

Char laid on her back with a sweet smile filled with anticipation. She laid there with the confidence that I did not possess. Maybe I would grow to be more confident with age. Besides, she was older than me by two years. Was I finally about to have sex? My mom told me it was sinful to have sex before marriage. But I could not keep Char waiting any longer or she would think I was some rookie.

I gently put one hand on her upper thigh. She grinned as if she was already enjoying it. I slid my hand inside her pants and rested it there. I thought I hope she is satisfied.

"Put them inside my panties," she said.

I guess I wasn't doing it right, after all. So I put my right hand inside her panties.

"Lower," Char said.

"Okay," I said reluctantly.

As my hand traveled down her vagina, I noticed moistness. It wasn't like running-water moistness, but she was wet. I had heard that a woman gets wet when she is ready to have sex, just like a man's penis gets hard.

I could not believe what was happening. She felt so good. As I pushed my middle finger inside of her, she let out a gentle moan. It felt like pushing my finger inside of an orange, but warmer. No, it was like a peach. Yeah, it felt like a warm peach. I looked up at Char's face and she had her eyes closed.

"Keep going," she instructed.

I kept moving my middle finger in and out of her as she continued to moan. Her face made an expression I had never seen before. She was in ecstasy. We soon heard a rumbling in the kitchen next door, and we both knew that it was our mothers wrapping up.

"We better stop," I said.

Char looked up at me and grabbed my shirt. She pulled me in close and kissed me on my cheek. I still had an erection, and I needed it to go down before our mothers walked in.

Char and I moved quickly to get the living room set up like it had been. Char grabbed all the blankets and pushed them into the closet.

"I will fold these later. Now go wash your hands," she said.

"Good idea."

I went to wash my hands with all kinds of thoughts swirling in my mind. I couldn't wait to tell Scooter that I touched Charlene's pussy. He was going to flip! I let the cold water running on my hands calm me, and my erection started to fade. Thank God.

When I got back to the living room, I grabbed my Gameboy and turned on Tetris. I acted like I had been playing all along when my mom walked in with Maxine behind her.

"You ready to go, boy?" my mom asked me.

"Yes Mother," I said back in a funny tone. She chuckled at the sound of "Mother."

I gave Ms. Maxine a hug and Char a hug. My mom and I headed out the door, and when I went to shut the door behind me, Charlene gave me a wink.

When I told Scooter the story, he said I was lying and if that was him, he would have stuck it in.

I shook that memory out of my head as I rang the doorbell. I waited for Evelyn to come to the door; it was taking her forever, it seemed. Maybe she's in the bathroom, I thought. I will give her a couple of minutes before I ring the doorbell again. I counted 60 seconds in my head and rang the doorbell again. Evelyn came to the door with exactly what she had on earlier. I didn't know what I was expecting.

"Hey, I didn't think you were coming," she said.

"I had to finish my chores. You know how Pops is."

"Come in the living room and watch TV with me."

She turned to walk to the living room and I followed behind her. I took a seat next to her on the living room couch. I started to feel my heart race and those same feelings started to come back from Charlene's house. The anxiety, nervousness, and sweating—I felt like an old war veteran having a flashback. Why was I feeling like this?

"Evelyn, I have something to tell you," I began.

"Sure, what is it? Is everything okay?" she asked with empathy.

"No. I never done this before," I said.

"Done what?" she asked.

"I'm nervous and have only had one other experience," I explained.

I launched into telling her everything about Charlene and me. How we used to play together in the sand box at age four and six. And then as we got older, how she started to develop a crush on me. Two summers ago, she insisted on playing house, but I really didn't want to.

"The thing is...I'm not ready to have sex. I don't even have any condoms," I said.

"Ha ha ha!" She laughed right in my face.

I told her something personal and she laughed in my face. I will never share anything with her again. How could she? I thought she was nicer than that.

"Is that it?" she finally said after catching her breath from laughing.

"Oh, that's funny to you, huh?" I said disappointedly.

"I'm sorry. I really am. I didn't mean to laugh. It's just that what made you think I was ready to have sex? We're thirteen, Ron!"

All of a sudden, a big relief swept over my body, as if all my worries had been cast away. I had not a care in the world. I was so thankful she spoke those words.

"Well, you were sweating me to come over. You kept talking about your parents working late and this and that," I said.

"I know, but that's because I wanted to have time to be alone with you. It doesn't mean I'm ready for all that. I'm not like those other fast girls, Ron. When the time is right, I will know. You will know. We don't have to have sex, but we could do other stuff." She leaned in and kissed me on the lips. And I returned the favor.

We finished watching my favorite movie, *Boyz N Da Hood*. It was getting late. I had to go home and Evelyn walked me to the door.

"I'm glad we had a chance a talk," she said.

"Me too," I said with a smile.

We kissed long and deep as if I was about to go out of town. "I really like you, Evelyn," I said. She smiled as I left to grab my bike from the side of the house. I went straight home because I had school tomorrow.

Reverend Brown lived two houses down from Evelyn. I heard him preach, and he was good, but my mom liked our church, Imani Baptist. He saw me leaving out of her house and waved me over. Reverend Brown was always giving someone unsolicited advice. He would tell you his opinion, whether you wanted to hear it or not.

"Hey Ronnie, you over there visiting Evelyn I see. You got permission to be over there?" he said.

"Yeah," I said, lying to him. He was always up in somebody's business. I wished he would mind his own.

"You like that girl, don't cha?" he said, with a grin as if he already knew the answer.

"Kinda…but it's not like that."

"Well, what's it like? Tell me."

"Look Rev. Brown, I gotta get home or I will get in trouble," I said, trying to get out of hearing his lecture.

"Just a couple of minutes—the streetlights not even on yet."

"All right, a couple of minutes."

"You know I'm an old man who done heard a lot and seen a lot. When I was young, I remember being in such a rush to grow up. You know, do grown things. Drive a fast car. But nobody ever sat me down and told me to enjoy being a kid because you only get one chance to be a kid, so you gotta have fun while you can."

It was almost as if he was inside my head, as if he knew what I was thinking. When he preached a sermon, this is what people would say about him: "Reverend Brown speaks to me and what I'm going through in my life. I feel spiritually fed after one of his sermons."

He continued, "I had my first child when I was seventeen. I wasn't ready to be nobody's daddy, but there I was, trying to be a father and still run the streets. That is probably why I go around preaching now. I wasn't even in love with my daughter's mom and we had to raise a child together. Imagine that.

"One thing I want you to know is if you lie down with a woman make sure you are in love with that woman. My uncle used to tell me this. Don't sleep with a woman you aren't willing to have a child with. That's the realest thing he taught me and those very words came back to haunt me. Use protection, boy, because getting a woman pregnant is NOT make-believe! Now go on, get! I have to watch my stories," Reverend Brown said, as if I interrupted his day to talk to him.

I was no fool and appreciated good advice. Maybe I would check Reverend Brown out at church next Sunday. It takes a village…

Chapter 14

Knuckle Up

I'm in junior high with a 'B plus' grade,
At the end of the day I don't hit the arcade,
I walk from school to my mom's apartment,
I got to tell the suckas everyday "don't start it,"
Cause where I'm at if your soft your lost,
To stay on course means to roll with force

—"Love Gonna Get'cha," **KRS-ONE**

Only three days left until school was out and I couldn't wait for the summer to be here. I was going to go swimming every day. I was thinking about taking the Junior Lifeguard Class so I could have the skills ready to be a lifeguard when I turned sixteen.

Some of my friends had nothing to do all summer and I felt bad for them. Every other summer, my parents would take me back to the East Coast to visit my relatives in Washington, D.C. I have also been in summer camps and college readiness programs like M.E.S.A. (Math Engineering Science Achievement).

My parents believed in exposing me to as many things as possible so I would be fully aware of the world out there, and that's why we traveled and tried different restaurants. They wanted me to picture myself being in college, so when it was time for me to go to college, it would not seem so daunting. I appreciated them for that.

"What are you going to do this summer?" I asked Scooter.

"Nothing—just sleep in. Maybe play some basketball at the park. What about you?"

"I'm going to do the junior lifeguard training. When I turn sixteen, it will be easier for me to become a lifeguard because they will already know my skills and that I am a solid hire," I explained.

"That's a good idea. You are the best swimmer I ever seen, dolphin Ron," he said, laughing.

"Don't call me that before it begins to stick," I said only partially joking.

"All right, I got you, but I'm impressed by you, bruh. You are always thinking ahead. I just don't want to get stuck on the block for the rest of my life because I didn't plan ahead."

"It's never too late to come up with a plan. Have you thought about how you want to spend your summer? Do you want to get a job like me? Do you want to prepare yourself for high school football? You are really good, Scooter. There are a bunch of football camps that would love to have someone with your speed and ability."

Scooter thought for a minute and replied, "Football camp sounds like it is right up my alley. Will you help me find a camp?"

"I got you, bruh. My mom and I will look up camps and call around. There are some low-cost ones and even free ones. You will not be stuck on the block this summer. Before you know it, I will be coming to your games when you play for the Niners," I said.

"Don't you mean Raiders?" Scooter said.

"It don't matter—I just want you to make it."

The bell rang and I dapped Scooter before he walked toward the gym. I had to go to Art class with Mr. Green. Mr. Green's class was the coolest because he had all kinds of fly stuff in his classroom. Mr. Green was a big fan of any movie or old-school TV shows that had to do with space. His wall was covered with everything—posters of *Star Trek* and *Star Wars,* and he was getting into this new TV show called *X Files.* The only one of those I watched was *Star Wars.* I thought that Luke Skywalker was dope and the fact that Darth Vader, who was the ultimate bad guy, was his father. Good versus evil, but the guy who represents evil is your dad? What a dilemma.

Mr. Green also had model cars, trucks, planes, and spacecrafts. Today we would be working on finishing our model cars. We had been working on them all semester long and most of us were done and others were just trying to put the finishing touches on their work.

I had chosen to put together a silver 1968 Super Sport Chevy Nova. It had a silver paint job and black racing stripes down the middle. It was the ultimate muscle car. The only thing I had left to do was put the wheels on.

Mr. Green's class was laid back because he wanted us to enjoy art and not think of art as boring. He would often ask us what we would like to do and how we would apply the skills we learned in life. I liked that about Mr. Green, and the fact that he was a highly respected black teacher. He played jazz in the background as we worked. How cool was that!

"Mr. Green, can we listen to some Sir Mix-a-Lot?" Randal asked.

"Not today, Randal. I need you all to concentrate and finish with the model car project. You will lose focus if I play rap music," Mr. Green said.

"Aww, please, Mr. Green. We only have a couple more days of school. We've been good all year," chimed in the class.

"Well, you are supposed to be good. Why do people always want rewards for doing things you are supposed to be doing? You are supposed to come to class on time. You are supposed to have all your materials and be ready to learn. You are supposed to be quiet whenever the teacher is speaking. These are the things you all are supposed to be doing. You want a reward for that?"

After his lecture, Mr. Green changed the radio station to KSOL for the last 15 minutes of class and we all were grooving to Bobby Brown, Whitney Houston, and Boyz II Men.

The bell rang and school was out. I was proud of my Chevy Nova and was showing it to everybody. We caught the 46 bus home, and as the bus sped down Mountain Boulevard and Fontaine, I passed the car around to my friends. Evelyn was sitting with Dee Dee. I locked eyes with her, as I got my model car back from James.

"Nice car, Ron," Evelyn said.

"Thank you," I said back.

All I needed was affirmation from a cutie. The homies' compliments were cool, but nothing like a compliment from the one you love.

The 46 bus got to our stop on 82nd and Hillside and we all got off and walked down Hillside on our way to 78th. As soon as I got home, I threw my books in my room and changed from my school clothes to play clothes. I grabbed my model car and started to head out before I ran into my father.

"Are you sure you want to take your model car out of the house? I know it took you some time putting it together," he said.

"Yeah, just for a minute. I'll be right back. You like it?"

"Yes. It looks great. It has lots of detail. Great work, son. Be careful and don't stay out with it for too long."

I grabbed my bike and my model car. I still had some showing off to do. I rode down 78th to get Scooter, James, and Victor. As we headed down the block and turned the corner, we almost ran into Tyreik, Tyrell, and few of their friends. They were all smoking cigarettes.

I was not really paying them any attention because I had my boys with me. I saw Manny standing with them, too. He waved me over. Manny knew I didn't like Tyreik and Tyrell.

"Let me see your ride, fam?" Manny said.

"All right, but be careful because the super glue is still drying on the wheels," I said to Manny, as I handed him my model car.

Manny looked at my car with great interest. He inspected it from top to bottom. Manny was still my friend, but I didn't like the fact that he sells dope or is the lookout or whatever. I didn't like the fact that his new friends are the same guys that have tormented us for years. It didn't sit well with me.

"This is fresh, Ron. I could see you in one of these one day," Manny said. That was the ultimate compliment.

I remember watching *The Karate Kid* and Mr. Miyagi telling Daniel, son, never take your eyes off the enemy, not even for one second. I was lost in a trance and still trying to figure out why Manny was hanging out with these guys.

As he handed back my model car, Tyrell's little brother, Tyreik, came on the side of me and slapped my model car out of my hands. The car hit the concrete with a thud. One of the tires and the back bumper came off. I reached down to retrieve my car and its pieces. I handed my model car to Scooter. I wasn't the type of kid to start fights, but I never backed away from them either. Maybe Tyreik thought I was a punk. Maybe he was trying to show off in front of his big brother.

"Man, I should I whip yo' ass for that!" I said with fire in my eyes.

"Run up then mark!" Tyreik said, without missing a beat.

As I started to put my bike against the wall, Tyreik rushed me and threw a punch. By this time, I was locked in, looking at him. I moved my head back, as I saw his fist coming toward my face in slow motion. It felt as if I was seeing his moves before he made them. His punch missed, but managed to brush my cheek. I grabbed Tyreik by his shirt and put him against the wall. I felt the strength of five boys surging through my scrawny arms.

I was motivated by anger, revenge, and hatred. I was tired and had enough. I gave Tyreik several rounds of right and left jabs. He had no defense for the onslaught that was taking place. I attacked his face first, giving him several shots to the eyes and nose, before I punched him in the stomach.

Thoughts of my father flashed in my head. The whippings he had given me over the years. I dodged Tyreik's blows like I dodged my dad's blows. I wasn't scared of any of the kids my age. If I could take a beating from a grown man, then kids my age could not affect me. Violence begets violence.

Tyreik was doubled over with a bloody nose when Scooter had nudged my shoulder to get my attention because I was still seeing red.

"Your bike, Ron!" Scooter yelled.

Tyrell was on my bike speeding up the street toward his apartment building on 77th.

"Why you didn't try and stop him?" I asked.

James, Scooter, and Manny were silent. Manny just shook his head, as he walked away. Tyreik ran toward his brother and didn't look back. He wouldn't want to look back after the beating he took.

Since none of my scrub friends would stop Tyrell from grabbing my bike, I could not rely on them to help me get it back. Manny was the one who waved me over in the first place. Why did I go over to him? Was all this a setup?

I ran straight home as fast as I could. When I got in the house, my father was in the living room just like he was when I left the house.

"What happened to your model car so quickly? I told you not to take it out of the house. What happened to you? What happened to your shirt?" he asked.

I had not noticed I had a few splotches of blood on my shirt from Tyreik's nose. I gave it to him good, but my bike was gone now. I told my dad everything. I spared no details. I told him they tried to distract me as they stole my bike. It was Tyrell.

"Did you win the fight, though?"

"Yes Dad."

"Did you lean into your punches like I showed you?"

"Yes Dad."

"My boy got hands! You might be the next Sugar Ray Leonard, boy!"

"Dad, umm…what about my bike?"

"I mean, you don't have a scratch on your face. Keeping it fresh for the dinner dance this weekend I see."

"*Dad*, my bike!"

"Oh yeah. I'm sorry. I'm just proud of you for defending yourself, son. This Tyrell cat, where does he stay?"

"At 77th Greenside."

"In the projects?"

"Yes Dad."

I could see my dad's wheels spinning for a second. He was trying to figure everything out. He was trying to put together a plan of action. Would he call the police? Would he tell my mother any of this or keep it between us?

My father jumped up abruptly and went into the back of the house. He returned with my aluminum bat, and now he had fire in his eyes.

"Dad, do you want me to come with you?" I asked.

"No son. You have done great tonight. Don't you worry. I'm going to get your bike back. Don't tell your mother any of this. I want you to take a shower and put on your pajamas." He then left the house in a wife beater, jeans, and running shoes. He looked like he was ready for war. Pops was a thug when he had to be.

It took something traumatic for my dad to be loving. That was just the way he was. Tonight I had his support and not his normal verbally abusive self. Had I not fought back, he would be kicking my ass. If I could take hits from a grown man, then I knew I could take hits from someone my age. I guess this is how we teach violence to our youth.

I was too overwrought to go to bed after my shower. I just looked out the window, wondering when my dad would be home. Those kids didn't respect elders. What if they jumped him? What if they sent my dad to the hospital and it was all my fault?

After a few more anxious distressed minutes, I heard my father call to me, "Ron, come here."

As I got to the front porch, I saw my dad standing there gloriously with my bike.

"Dad, how'd you—"

"It doesn't matter. Tyrell will never bother you again. Lock your bike up in the back."

"Thanks, Dad," I said and gave him the biggest hug ever. He was proud of me and I was ever so proud that he was my father.

As I headed to the backyard, I couldn't help but think that my father was sometimes black superman.

Chapter 15

Time to Cut a Rug

Now your party wasn't jumping and your DJ was
weak

Instead of dope beats, he was spinnin' them Z's

All the fly girls who came with a beat in mind

They all up against the wall like a welfare line

Do you think for one minute that this is it?

Your party is bogus, yo' it ain't legit

You better PUT on the hammer, and you will be
rewarded

My beat is ever boomin,' and you know I get it started

Get it started!

—"Let's Get It Started," **MC Hammer**

It was the perfect night for the eighth-grade dinner dance and I was as nervous as a hen in a slaughterhouse. My mother had taken me to buy a nice suit from the Burlington Coat Factory. She said I could wear the suit at the dinner dance, but to be careful in it because it would be my future church suit, too. Oh great, I thought.

Evelyn and I had decided on what color my tie should be. Well, we didn't actually decide together. She basically told me what color tie I was going to get and I got it. I have to remember this for the future. The woman usually knows best. What's the sense of arguing? She had more experience with this than me. She had probably been thinking about dinner dances, proms, and weddings her whole life.

I laid out my suit on the bed and hoped in the shower. Put a fresh coat of Murray's wave grease in my hair. My waves were poppin'! I had worn my wave cap all day. The only problem was I had a line across my forehead where the wave cap was. The wave cap had put a crease in my forehead. I never wore my wave cap that long in my life. I hoped I wasn't going to roll up to the dance with this permanent line across my forehead. That would be a travesty.

"Yo' Dad!"

"Wassup? When do you think you will be ready to go?" my father asked.

"Bout 30 more minutes," I replied.

My father was going to be our chauffeur for the evening. I was happy because he could coach me on what to say and how to be in a formal setting. I couldn't believe it, but my dad was going to be my dating mentor.

The line on my forehead was already starting to fade. I was stressing out for nothing. I put my new black suit on and tied my burgundy tie. I knew how to tie a tie because of my many years going to church. That was my training.

I knocked on the door to my parents' room to make sure no one was in there. It was empty, so I proceeded to my parents' full-length mirror. I took one look in the mirror and was impressed with what I saw. I'm not conceited or anything like that, but I was cleaner than the board of health!

I wanted to practice what I was going to say to Evelyn. I wanted to be smooth as silk. I wanted to be the definition of cool. Tonight I would be a young Billy Dee Williams.

"You look stunning this evening."

"No, you look marvelous this evening."

"No, you look tantalizing this evening." I couldn't say this one. I didn't even know what it means. I laughed at myself. I was taking this way too seriously.

"Ron, just be confident, playboy," I said to myself nervously.

"May I have this dance?"

"Would you like to shake a tail feather?"

"Let's cut a rug."

What is this, the fifties? She would laugh in my face. No she wouldn't. Evelyn was a sweetheart. My internal dialogue was telling me to chill out. I had never been to a dinner dance. Think of it as prom practice. By the time prom rolls around, you will be a professional ladies' man.

"My dear, what a lovely—" my mom began, suppressing a chuckle.

"What on earth are you doing, Ron?"

"Oh, I was just practicing a few lines."

"For what?"

"Just so I don't seem like a rookie…you know?"

"But you are," my mom teased.

"I know, but I don't want to come off as such."

"Look Ron, just be yourself. It's just like anything else in life. Always be yourself. Never try to be someone you are not. You are a nice guy and handsome I might add. Nobody can be you, but you. Try being yourself. You will be good at it."

"Thanks Mom."

"I thought I was the only one in this house who talked to themselves. I guess it runs in the family," she said and winked before she laughed.

"Well, at least I don't ask myself questions and answer them. Now that's psycho," I said and winked back.

"Good one. Your father wants to know if you are almost ready."

"Yep. Give me like 5 minutes."

My mother left the bedroom to allow me to collect my thoughts. She was right. I'm just going to be myself. Being myself was what got Evelyn to say yes in the first place.

I stepped into the living room and my father instantly put down the TV remote and stood up. He looked me up and down and smiled the biggest smile I had ever seen.

"Boy, you are sharp!" he said.

"Thanks Pops."

"You are sharper than a thumb tack!"

I was excited about the evening. My parents told me I looked good and I was just a reflection of them. I hugged my mom and she told me to have a good time. My father reminded me to grab Evelyn's corsage out of the refrigerator. A corsage is a small bouquet of flowers worn on a woman's dress or around the wrist. The man usually brought it to his date. I didn't know what a corsage was before tonight. My mom told me all about it.

As we stepped off the porch and onto the driveway, I noticed the car had a nice shine to it. My father had the car detailed for my big night. I looked up the block and saw Scooter in his gray suit. I must admit he was looking good, too.

"Go say hi real quick and then we gotta go. Rule number one is never be late picking up your date."

"I'll be right back," I said and hurried over to say hello to Scooter.

Scooter had finally mustered up the courage to ask Dee Dee out. Scooter's father, Tony, was going to drive him to the dance.

"Well, would you look at us...We look like some ballers, don't we?" Scooter proclaimed.

"Yes, we do." I admitted.

Scooter's mom and dad were outside looking us over and complimenting us. Scooter's mom, Delores, took out a disposable camera and snapped a few pictures of us.

"I'll see you up there, GQ."

"See you in a few, playboy."

Evelyn was just around the corner, so it would have been bad if we were late. My father pulled up in front of the house with his shiny almost-new Volkswagen Jetta. We both got out of the car and walked to her house. My father had his camera in hand.

I knocked on the door with butterflies in my stomach. Evelyn's mom, Adrienne, answered the door.

"Hi Ms. Hughes," I said.

"Hello, Ronald."

"Good afternoon, Adrienne," my dad said.

"Good afternoon, Ronald Senior. Won't you two come in? You look great, Ronald. Evelyn will be out in a second. She's almost ready."

Ms. Hughes left to go get Evelyn. We took a seat on the couch. I was anxious and ready to get the night going. My palms were moist and I made sure that my father was focused on the TV when I wiped my hands on the couch cushions.

When Evelyn entered the room, it was like the world stopped. All I could focus on was her beauty. I had never seen her with makeup on. She described the dress to me, but not in this detail. The dress hugged her nice booty and her curves. He cleavage showed just enough to make the mind wonder, and my mind was wondering. She could stop a parade in that dress. She could stop a herd of buffalo in that dress. She could stop a war in that dress. She looked damn good!

I stood up. "Wow! Oh my God, wow!" Not exactly like I practiced, but oh well.

"Well, good afternoon to you, too," she said.

"I'm sorry… You look amazing, Evelyn. I got you this," I said and proceeded to hand her the corsage.

"You have to put that thing on her," my dad explained.

"Oh yeah," I said.

I delicately pinned the white and burgundy corsage to Evelyn's dress. Her dress went perfectly with the corsage. I had picked this one myself.

"Thank you. It's wonderful," Evelyn said.

Our parents snapped pictures while I was putting her corsage on and we took a few pictures in front of Evelyn's fireplace. We would have all night to take pictures, so Evelyn and I both hugged Ms. Hughes and headed out. I made sure to get the door for my date, exiting the house and getting in the car. My dad had given me a few tips and they were paying off already. We both smiled on our way to the Berkeley Marina.

The dance was going to be held at a fancy restaurant called Hs. Lordship. Hs. Lordship was located on the water of the Berkeley Marina. The sun was still out when we got there, so we took more photos by the water.

It was nice to see all my classmates in their suits and nice dresses. All of the girls' hair was on point and all the fellas had nice haircuts, fresh from the barbershop. My wave cap line was completely gone now and I was thankful.

"Look at the whole gang," James said.

"We look like mobsters out of a sixties movie," Scooter said.

"I never seen all of us dress so fly. We look good!" I said.

"I bet you haven't worn that suit since your Quinceañera, huh?" Scooter said to Victor.

"Quinceañeras are for girls, you idiot!" Victor replied.

"Exactly!" Scooter quipped back. We all laughed.

Victor was so cool and nothing seemed to bother him. Besides, he knew he looked good. He had on a tan-colored suit with a small embroidered Mexican flag on his brown tie. His hair was faded on the side and spiked up top. He must have used some kind of gel to get it to stay up like that.

James had on a navy-blue suit and black shoes. He was already a good-looking boy, but his suit accentuated his attributes.

"Well, you look like you work for the Black Muslim Bakery… You be on the corner like "bean pie, my brotha," he said.

We laughed hard. "Easy on the black jokes, man," Scooter said.

"You guys are always getting on me about my Mexican heritage. I'm just defending myself," Victor shot back.

"You right, you right, us black and brown peeps need to stick together. Let's party tonight!" Scooter said.

Evelyn and her crew of girls were snapping pictures and smiling and complimenting one another. My anxiety was abating and I couldn't wait to dance with her.

We took pictures and laughed for a couple of hours and then folks started to migrate to the front of Hs Lordships as they propped open the doors and allowed us to come in.

The first thing that caught your attention was the décor. It was a ballroom like something out of Cinderella. The place was decorated in gold and silver. Nice linens everywhere and a big banner that said, "King Estates Dinner Dance."

The ballroom was sectioned off with the food being on one side. The back had circular tables set up for eating and the front had a nice dance floor.

The food smelled amazing. You had so many options to choose from. Fettuccine Alfredo, roasted chicken, seasoned vegetables, lasagna and garlic bread, and cheesecake for dessert.

The crew sat together with our dates and ate, joked, and laughed, until it was time to get on the dance floor.

"Can I have this dance?" I asked Evelyn smoothly.

"Why certainly," she said, with a British accent, and we giggled and hit the dance floor. The crew followed me with their dates. All they needed was someone to start it off.

We danced until we were dripping with sweat. I was busy doing the Running Man. I looked to my left and Scooter and Victor were doing the Roger Rabbit. I had to get in on that because my Roger Rabbit was much doper than theirs.

The DJ was spinning all the hit records. He put on "Ain't Gon' Hurt Nobody" by Kid N' Play and we all started doing the Kid N' Play like we were in the movie, *House Party*. Evelyn was my partner and we both smiled as I grabbed my partner for the do-si-do.

Before we knew it, the DJ started spinning a few slow jams and that's how we knew the night was coming to an end. The DJ played "Forever My Lady" by Jodeci, and I could hear all the girls scream, "That's my jam," as they ran onto the dance floor. The girls who didn't have dates just danced with each other.

I looked over to see Victor dancing with Marisela, James dancing with Porsha, Scooter dancing with Dee Dee, and of course I had my Evelyn. She sang so gently in my ear. She didn't seem to mind all the sweat coming from my shirt either.

As the song concluded, we took a few more photos and headed out front to wait for our rides. A few of our classmates left in limousines, but none of my crew could afford those. We would save that for prom night.

As my father pulled up to the front of Evelyn's house, we both looked at each other as if it had been the best night of our lives. I walked her to the door, kissed her, and told her I would see her at school on Monday.

I walked back to my dad's car, feeling like the man.

He asked me, "Well, how was it?"

"Only one word to describe it," I replied.

"And what's that?"

"Magical!"

Chapter 16

Nothing but a Hoodlum

A mellow type of fellow that's laid back
Back in the days he was nothing like that
I remember when he used to fight every day
What grownups would tell him he would never obey
He wore his pants hanging down and his sneakers
untied
And a Rasta-type Kangol tilted to the side
Around his neighborhood people treated him bad
And said he was the worst thing his mom's ever had
They said that he will grow up to be nothing but a
hoodlum
Or either in jail, or someone would shoot him

—"Vapors," **Biz Markie**

Last night's dinner dance was so fun that I had completely forgotten I lived in the hood. Living below the poverty line was one thing, but our neighborhood was more like a community. It was like a family.

We were still boycotting the liquor store on Hillside for the store owner pulling a gun on me. When I wanted to buy something or play video games, I went to the liquor store on MacArthur or Bancroft. The Bancroft liquor store was near the 77th Greenside Projects. I knew Manny was going to be on the corner.

Scooter, Victor, and James came by my house early that Sunday morning. We had planned on going to the store and then to Arroyo Park to run plays for the basketball tournament we would enter in this summer. We wanted to win another championship badly.

As we approached 77th and Greenside on our bikes, we all zeroed in on Manny. He wasn't at his normal spot looking out for the cops. He was with the other Dope Boys who actually did the crack dealing. I looked back at the corner stoop where Manny usually was, and another kid from the around the way was posted there. Maybe Manny had graduated to selling crack. This wasn't the type of graduation I had in mind for him.

"Should we say wassup to Manny?" I asked.

"And tell him about the dance last night?" James said.

"I'm not sure what good that will do. He don't want to hear about no stinking dinner dance. That fool is trying to get paid. I don't blame him. Tired of being broke," Victor said.

"You're right. Manny is not going to want to hear about how fresh we were dressed or how much fun we had," I said.

None of us wanted to rub in the fact that we had a blast at the dinner dance, but we felt something was missing from our crew now that Manny was gone. Making money is intoxicating, but I didn't think Manny fully understood the significance of selling crack cocaine in our community. We had seen first-hand teenage crackheads, mother and father crackheads, and even pregnant crackheads. Manny was making matters worse by contributing to the destruction of Oakland.

I still liked Manny and wished that we were friends, but was not happy with the decisions he was making. I tried to look at it from Manny's point of view. What if my back was against the wall? What if my mother struggled to raise me and my siblings? What if I knew a way to help my mother with the bills even though it was illegal? Nope, I still wouldn't do it, too much at stake. I care about my life and future. When did Manny stop caring?

"He is helping to destroy our community," I finally said.

"You're just jealous he is stacking paper," Scooter said.

"No, I'm not. My time will come. Besides, I want money, but I don't want to die for it."

"Look at Manny's clothes. He went from rocking Pro Wings to Jordan's in a week. You have to wonder what it would be like to buy whatever you want...or to help moms with PG&E. If you haven't thought about it, then you are lying," Victor said.

"Thinking about it is one thing, but dealing death to pregnant women is another issue. Ron's right. Oakland has enough issues with prostitution and violence, but crack has made it a hundred times worse. I'm going say wassup to Manny and keep it moving," James said.

We rode to where Manny was standing with the other young D Boys.

"Wassup Manny," we all said and gave the wassup head nod.

Manny gave a quick head nod and continued talking to the rest of his new gang. He barely acknowledged us. Just that fast, within a matter of a week, Manny was turning his back on his crew that he had known since he could walk. Manny had no time for us. Manny had lost his way.

We rode off fast because we weren't supposed to be hanging out on 77th Greenside anyway. We set our bikes down on the side of the basketball court.

"Let me see the ball, James Worthy," Scooter said.

"I get the first shot. My ball, my rules," James said. James took the basketball out of his backpack and ran dribbling up to the free throw line. He set his feet, took the shot, and drained the jumper, nothing but net.

"Your first shot tells you how your game is going to be that day, whether you are hot or cold. You feel me?" James said, sounding too cocky for my taste.

"No, it doesn't. What about that game Tim Hardaway was 0 to 7 in the first half, but finished the game with 28 points?" Scooter said.

"Good point, Scoot. Let me show you what I'm talking about, though. Let's play 21," James said and took the ball to the top of the key.

The first person to score 21 points wins. When you score a basket, you get a chance to add to your score with free throws. We played that you had to shoot your free throws from the three-point arc to make the game more challenging.

We played four games. James won two and Scooter and I won one game apiece. Maybe James was on to something with that hitting the first shot jazz because his jumper was wet. Basketball wasn't really Victor's sport, but he played along to appease us.

Scooter helped us remember the main plays we used to run during summer league. He was the coach's son after all. There was a lot of pressure on Scooter. He was our point guard and he was responsible for remembering plays and calling them out at the right time.

James could play point guard or shooting guard. I was a shooting guard until my handles got better. We had so much energy and we were thankful to have outlets for using all that energy.

We stayed at the park until late afternoon. By this point, I was tired and hungry and could feel my stomach starting to hurt.

"Man, I wonder what's for dinner tonight. I'm starving like Marvin," I said to no one in particular.

"Me too, bruh. We been at the park for hours," Scooter said.

Riding our bikes up 77th, we could feel the spring breeze and it helped to cool us off. I was happy that we went over our plays. I liked being prepared, but was not prepared for what I saw next.

"Damn, look at the Greenside PJ's," James said.

I hadn't seen it before James said something, but I looked up in time to see Manny with his hands cuffed behind his back being stuffed into the back of a police car.

We had come to a stop at this point. We were aghast. Our mouths were wide open, trying to figure out how this had happened so quickly. We knew how it happened. Manny went after the quick money and ignored all the consequences affiliated with hustling.

"Wow, like father like son," Scooter said.

"Shut up, blood."

I was so angry with Scooter for saying that I pushed him. I pushed him so hard that I almost knocked him off his bike. When Scooter gathered himself, he charged after me. I quickly knocked his hands down and put him in a headlock.

"Stop fighting! This isn't going to get Manny out of jail," Victor said, and he was right.

I think we were all frustrated we couldn't save him. Or maybe we felt responsible since we got mad at Manny for stealing the water gun. Had we not gotten so mad, maybe he would have still wanted to hang out with us. Whatever the case, this was going to have to be a lesson that Manny learned on his own.

Chapter 17

I Call Your Name

Woke up in the morning, put my arm to the side

Didn't feel your body near me, so I opened my eyes

Then I pulled back the sheets but I forgot it was cold

So I slipped into the slippers and I put on my robe

Took a journey to the bathroom to wash my face

The house is kinda quiet, not a sound in the place

And then I thought: wait a minute, where is my

woman?

She up and left the house and didn't leave a note or

nothin?

I rushed out the bathroom to check the house

Not a peep, a sound, not even a mouse

I said: man, she up and cold left me

Huh, where could she be?

I call your name I call your name

—"I Call Your Name," **Dangerous Dame**

One of my best friends was going to Juvie and all I could do was sit there and watch. I tried to tell him to stay away from Greenside. Manny was so hard-headed sometimes. Why didn't he just listen to me for once? To top it off, Evelyn was leaving for the summer. Wait, was today the day she was leaving? I couldn't imagine not telling her goodbye before she left. I would be devastated, but maybe she was still at home. I called her house, but her auntie picked up the phone, talking about who is this and how you get this number. I hung up. I would just go by her house and see if she was with Dee Dee.

I rode my bike to her house and threw it down on the front lawn. I jumped off my bike and rang the doorbell. Her little brother, Boo, answered the door.

"Wassup Boo. Is your sister here? I wanted to tell her bye before she left," I said.

"Wassup Ronnie. You just missed her. She went to the mall with Dee Dee. You should be able to find them, though," Boo said.

"Thanks man." I gave him dap and hopped on my bike and sped out of there.

I was flying down Hillside, and when I got to the mall, I could see Dee Dee and Evelyn about to walk into Mervyn's.

"Hi Evelyn—last-minute shopping, huh?"

"There go your stalker!" Dee Dee said.

"Shut up, Dee Dee. Ain't nobody even talking to you," I said.

"Dee Dee, could you give us a minute?" Evelyn said.

Dee Dee started walking in a different direction so that I and Evelyn could talk. I was glad that she didn't put up a fight.

"Sooooo, what are you going to do this summer without me?" Evelyn said with a smirk.

"I'm going to get a job working for the Oakland mayor's summer youth program. I already got my application in. Saving up for that 5.0 Mustang thang," I said in a matter-of-fact way.

"What are you getting a Mustang for? You want to be in those sideshows and get yourself killed?" she said.

"Maybe you can ride shotgun while I'm doing my thang," I said, trying to sound cooler than I really was.

"So we can have the police chasing us, or better yet, run into a building and die from the impact. I don't think so. I plan on becoming a surgeon and swinging doughnuts is not going to get me there," Evelyn said.

"But you always are on the Ave. watching the sideshows with your girls. You wouldn't spin one figure-eight with me?" I said, pleading with her.

"I know, but that's because there is nothing better to do. See, this is the hood and sideshows are a hood pastime. I don't plan on living in the hood for the rest of my life. You feel me?"

Maybe I was taking a short-sighted approach to life. What was my end game? If I couldn't see past the hood, then

I would be trapped. Despite all the drama, fights, and ignorance that can take place in East Oakland, there is no place I would rather be. I never thought about leaving the hood, but that's what people did when they made a little money. They would buy a nice house in the hills. That's what I would do. Buy a nice house in the Oakland Hills. That way, I could come down to the flatlands of East Oakland whenever I wanted to be around some realness. But would the hood label me a sellout for moving? Would I have to deal with survivor's remorse?

"That's why I like you, Evelyn, getting me to expand my thinking. I'm still gonna get that Mustang 5.0, though. I gotta have it. What are you gonna do this summer?" I then asked.

"I'm going to miss you, but I need a vacation. I'm looking forward to going to Louisiana to hang out with my cousins. I might join a prep squad out there."

A prep squad was kind of like being a cheerleader, but much cooler. Their outfits were cooler and they didn't have any soft cheers like "V-I-C-T-O-R-Y, V-I-C-T-O-R-Y" or "GO TEAM, GO," which sounded corny next to the prep squad. Oakland had a prep squad called the Oaktown Steppers. It was almost like watching a college sorority.

Evelyn was cut from a different cloth than these other hood rats. My baby was sophisticated and she wanted me to aim high.

"You're not like the other girls around here. That's what I like about you. You get me to see outside of the 700 zone. I never thought about going to college before and now I think it's a possibility, despite how I feel about how they never educate us about what black folks have contributed to this country," I explained.

She listened and took it all in before replying, "We can't count on the teachers in these public schools to give a damn about our African ancestry. They are too busy trying to get us to pass these stinking standardized tests. We have to learn about our heritage on our own. Just like how the Black Panthers had Saturday school for the community back in the day."

She was giving me game. That's what the OGs said when somebody was dropping knowledge. She was gaming me up. I always liked this side of her, the fact that she was both street and book smart.

"Unless you want to end up in jail like your friend Manny or shot like Tyrell—pick one," she said.

She knew how to break it all down to help me understand. Just in case I was missing the point, Evelyn was there to underline the meaning for me.

I couldn't feel sorry for Tyrell because of him trying to steal my bike and all. I would not wish getting shot on anyone. Tyrell came from a family where abuse was a normal thing. There was a cycle of abuse. Tyrell acted on what he learned in his household and neighborhood. Tyrell was a victim of circumstance. Being in the wrong place at the wrong time, your life could change in an instant in East Oakland. You have to be aware of everything around you in The Town. Like Coach Tony would tell me, "Keep your head on a swivel or get knocked down!"

I made it through another school year and couldn't wait to start high school. The school system is crazy that way. You pay dues all through elementary school only to start over again in middle school. You go through hell and high water in middle school only to start over again as a freshman in high school. As soon as you master high school and you're feeling like a king as a senior, then you are snatched off your perch and have to start over again in college.

That's the cycle of education while getting the white man's education. That's what black folks lost after Brown vs. Board of Education. Black folks educate black folks better than white folks could ever imagine. The irony is that you need the white man's diploma in order to make it in life.

I hadn't seen Manny in a couple of months now. His mama, Ms. Lewis, said to leave him in to teach him a lesson. I thought the real reason behind not going to get her only son was because she was tired of dealing with all the drama Manny had in store for her. Or was she tired of having to raise the boy? I wondered if she was tired of all the extra money Manny was giving her when he was dealing.

Manny was in a juvenile detention center off 150th in San Leandro. San Leandro was the neighboring city next to Oakland. If the juvenile had a serious offense or was a repeat offender, then they would send them to the Youth Authority Camp, also known as Y.A.

I wrote him a few letters. I remember the first one:

Dear Manny,

I wanted to write to you to let you know to keep your head held high. The summer is almost here and the 700 Bike Crew is missing you.

In church, my preacher said that you can atone for your mistakes. If you truly repent for your mistakes, then ALL will be forgiven.

Tyrell got shot and is paralyzed from the waist down. He wasn't even the intended target. I guess a trigger's got no heart, like Spice One said in that one song.

Scooter, Victor, and James are still the same. Victor might be moving to San Jose because his dad got a job out there. The last sideshow the bike crew went to was a disaster because this lady got hit on the corner. She didn't get out of the way fast enough, her bad.

I'm not even mad at you. I understand why you were doing what you were doing, but when you get out, I want to show you a better way. Do you remember you said, "Let the preacher preach on Sundays?" But I have to tell you that there is a way out. I know there is a difference between slow money and fast money. You still get the same amount of girls, but the fast money will have you locked up. Just look at Cadillac Todd.

Anyway, what they feeding ya'll in there? Do you get to shoot hoops? What's your release date? This isn't a goodbye, but I'll see you later (I got this from some sappy movie).

Audi 5000 (Peace),

Ronald A.

I felt better after I sent the letter to Manny. I wondered if he would write me back or think I was just some dork. Your life could change in the blink of eye in the hood.

When age sixteen finally rolled around, I never did get that 5.0 Drop Mustang. My dad took me to get a used Volkswagen Jetta. I don't even think the car was capable of swinging a full doughnut. It was probably better that way.

The 700 crew was still front and center in my ride. You could catch us in Berkeley, Hayward, Richmond, Vallejo, San Francisco, San Leandro, or wherever there were girls. Even though it was a Volkswagen, we rode it like a Benz.

People say Ron you are wise beyond your years. What does that really mean? Do I have an old soul? Was I growing up too fast? Am I a product of my environment? No one knows the answer to these philosophical questions.

All I know is to drink lots of water, look both ways before crossing the street, and get your butt in the house before the streetlights come on. And don't let nobody ride your bike!

Credits: Discography

"Ain't No Future In Yo' Frontin', **by MC Breed**, 1991, *MC Breed & DFC*

"Alleyway," **by The Delinquents**, 1995, *The Alleyway*

"Angel," **by Anita Baker**, 1983, *The Songstress*

"City of Dope, **by Too Short**, *Life Is...Too Short*

"Dig It," **by The Coup**, 1993, *Kill My Landlord*

"Don't Give Me No Bammer Weed," **by R.B.L. Posse**, 1992, *A Lesson to Be Learned*

"Hood Took Me Under," **by MC Eiht**, 1992, *Music to Drive By*

"I Call Your Name," **by Dangerous Dame**, 1991, *Powers That Be*

"Let's Get It Started," **by MC Hammer**, 1988, *Let's Get Started*

"Let's Talk About Sex," **by Salt-N-Pepa**, 1991, *Black Magic*

"Love's Gonna Get You," **by KRS-One**, 1990, *Edutainment*

"The Old School," **by Seagram**, 1994, *Reality Check*

"Sideshow," **by Richie Rich**, 1990, *Don't Do It*

"Sunshine in the O," **by 3X Krazy**, 1995, *Sicko*

"Vapors," **by Biz Markie**, 1988, *Cold Chillin'*

"Ward of the State," **by Askari X**, 1992, *Ward of the State*

"We Will Rock You," **by Queen**, 1977, *News of the World*

Credits: Books

"Nikki-Rosa," *Black Feeling, Black Talk, Black Judgment, by Nikki Giovanni, 1968*

"We Real Cool," *The Bean Eaters*, by Gwendolyn Brooks, 1960

References

Ellison, R., 1947, *Invisible Man*, Random House Inc., New York, NY

Wright, R., 1940, *Native Son*, HarperCollins Publishers, New York, NY

About the Author

Robert Mossi Alexander was born in San Francisco in 1978 and moved to East Oakland in 1980. The experiences that Robert had growing up in the Bay Area shaped who he is as a person. Robert loved his childhood so much that he wanted to share it with the world.

Robert has been an academic counselor for more than fifteen years. His passion is helping historically underrepresented students succeed in college. Robert is an author, counselor, father, teacher, and life coach.

His dream is to help increase critical literacy and critical thinking skills for youth of color. Robert envisions as his role as an educator to expose youth from marginalized communities to the importance of higher education.

CPSIA information can be obtained
at www.ICGtesting.com
Printed in the USA
FSHW022019120719
59965FS